TRUE TALES
of
GHOSTLY
encounters

Also from the Files of FATE Magazine

Mysteries of the Deep
Frank Spaeth, editor

Psychic Pets & Spirit Animals
FATE Magazine

Strange but True
Corrine Kenner and Craig Miller, editors

TRUE TALES
of
GHOSTLY
encounters

Compiled & Edited by
Andrew Honigman

Llewellyn Publications
Woodbury, Minnesota

57141061

133. 1
TRU

First Edition
Eighth Printing, 2010

Previously titled *My Proof of Survival: Personal Accounts of Contact with the Hereafter* 2003.

Book design and project management by Joanna Willis
Book layout and editing by Andrew Honigman
Cover art ©PhotoDisc
Cover design by Kevin R. Brown

Library of Congress Cataloging-in-Publication Data
My proof of survival: personal accounts of contact with the hereafter / compiled & edited by Andrew Honigman.—1st ed.
    p.   cm.
  ISBN 13: 978-0-7387-0989-5
  ISBN 10: 0-7387-0989-1
    1. Future life. 2. Spiritualism. I. Honigman, Andrew, 1970–

  BF1311.F8M9 2003
  133.9'01'3—dc22

                            2003058849

Llewellyn Publications
A Division of Llewellyn Worldwide, Ltd.
2143 Wooddale Drive, Dept. 978-0-7387-0989-5
Woodbury, MN 55125-2989, U.S.A.
www.llewellyn.com
Llewellyn is a registered trademark of Llewellyn Worldwide, Ltd.
Printed in the United States of America

Contents

Apparitions 35
Return Visits by the Departed

Warnings 69
Saved by the Dead

Unfinished Business 89
Promises Kept; Tasks Completed after Death

Children and Ghosts   123
Spiritual Experiences of Young People

Visions   145
Personal Experiences of the Afterlife and Past-Life Memories

From Long Ago   165
Stories from the Past

Companions   189
Cases of Animal Survival

Curtain Calls   255
Supernatural Communication at the Moment of Death

Blessings   273
Gifts from the Departed

Introduction

"What happens after we die?"

This is one of the great questions of human existence. Like that other great question—"Why are we here?"—it has no single accepted answer.

For many, the survival (or rebirth) of the individual is a deeply held matter of religious faith. For others, the notion of an immortal soul is nonsense. The wisest religious and scientific thinkers agree that they may never find mutually satisfactory answers to such questions. Faith either makes sense or it does not, depending on one's disposition, and science has little to say one way or the other with any great confidence.

Is there any way out of this impasse?

When considering this question, it is important to note that many millions of people, from the beginning of recorded history, have reported significant experiences that gave them reason to believe in the survival of the individual after death.

Departed souls have contacted the living, have been seen and heard, and have given reports on their condition. Persons on the brink of death (or beyond) have returned with information on what they saw and experienced. "Past lives" have been recalled, and sometimes verified with astonishing accuracy.

FATE magazine was founded in 1948 to provide a forum for extraordinary experiences of all kinds. (The first issue featured Kenneth Arnold's report on his "flying saucer" sighting of the previous year—the sighting that marked the beginning of the UFO era.) Contributions from readers have always featured prominently in the magazine's content, beginning in the earliest days with a section called "True Mystic Experiences." In 1954, the editors introduced "My Proof of Survival," a department dedicated to reader's reports bearing on the subject of life after death.

In the forty-nine years since its debut, *FATE* has published more than two thousand stories of this nature, all attested to be true by their authors. The *FATE* archives represent a tremendous resource for anyone interested in the question of afterlife survival—whether looking for evidence, or simply curious about what people believe and why.

Some of the best stories from our archives are presented in this book.

Messages
Communication from the Other Side

What do the departed have to say to the living? Sometimes, the simple fact that a loved one is able to communicate from the other side is enough.

In these stories, *FATE* readers report messages of love, encouragement, and hope from the hereafter. (There are also some humorous accounts indicating the dead aren't above taking offense at statements by their survivors.) These communications take varied and sometimes unexpected forms—everything from personal visits, to written messages, to levitating objects, and more.

Night of the "Living"

Our family friend of forty years died on December 3, 1993. His name was Joe G. and he lived in Sedona, Arizona.

After his memorial service, I spent time at his condo packing and throwing things out. As I weeded through his possessions, I apologized out loud to Joe for having to do it. Between tears and laughter, I teased him about how much of a pack rat he had become. In his drawers and closets were every bag and box that had come his way in the two and a half years he had lived there. Two boxes in particular were just the right size for packing dishes. So I packed them up and left for lunch.

Knowing that only the property management company and I had access to the condo helped me reason away what happened next. Upon returning I found that on each of the boxes were letters in black magic marker, written in a shaky scrawl that spelled out the word "living." *Well*, I thought, *I must have missed that when I packed the boxes.*

After more packing and cleaning, eight o'clock rolled around and I left for dinner. I couldn't chase away my anxiety about returning after dark to stay there by myself. But I went back anyway. The same two boxes were still in the hallway, but someone or something had written "living" two more times. Now there were four words that I hadn't seen before.

As much as I tried to convince myself that those words were there before I left, I didn't believe it. I still had the feeling I was not alone. So I grabbed my things and stayed at a motel seven miles down the road.

I headed back to the condo the next morning thinking how silly I had been to spend the extra money. I was sure it was just my imagination.

That morning the sun was shining through the windows and the place looked really cheery. Everything was just where I had left it. Heaving a sigh of relief, I put down my purse and walked to the center of the living room to finish packing. What I saw next took my breath away. On six of the boxes I found the word "living" written very clearly in black magic marker.

I knew every single one of those boxes had been unmarked, because I had examined them thoroughly after the previous day's scare. I truly believe Joe was there to let me know that, even though he didn't get to say goodbye in person, he was still near, and still alive.

L. M. Nickerson
Sedona, Arizona
January 1998

Don't Worry

I was born on September 13, 1949, without hope of survival. Low-birthweight babies have a difficult time, often living only weeks or months.

My mother was six months pregnant when I was born, and I weighed only one pound, seven ounces. The medical professionals were not encouraged, saying that no baby had ever survived at that hospital weighing so little.

One morning my mother was lying in bed at the hospital, depressed and worried. She didn't want to believe the doctors and nurses. Then, two men sat on the edge of the bed. One was her father. The other, a handsome man whom she had seen only in photographs, was her father-in-law. Both of these men were dead. Her father died two years before I was born, and her father-in-law died when my father was ten.

She told me she wasn't afraid. "I was surrounded by a peaceful feeling—something I couldn't explain."

My grandfather told her, "Don't worry or listen to your doctors—they are wrong. Your baby will survive and grow up to be a wonderful daughter and beautiful child."

The doctors and nurses noticed a change in her attitude after this. To their minds, she wasn't facing facts. They explained that the odds were a million to one I would survive; even if I did, they told her, I would have many health problems. They even told her to pray that I would die so I wouldn't suffer.

My mother smiled and kept her positive attitude. I kept fighting, and the doctors shook their heads in amazement. Mother left the hospital and walked back every day to stare at me through the glass wall. Back then you weren't allowed to hold a baby; parents couldn't even enter the premature section of the nursery.

I gained weight slowly. The tubes were removed, one by one, and I began to look like a normal baby. Mother told me she could have held me in the palm of her hand when I was born.

On Christmas Day, after more than three months in the hospital, I was brought home. I weighed five pounds.

My grandfathers delivered a message, and my mother believed them.

Nancy Duci Denofio
Glenville, New York
February 1994

The Doxology

My mom and dad visited me in California in the mid-1960s. I took them to a New Thought church. It was their first experience with this kind of service, and they both loved it, especially the hymn called "The Doxology." Having been Catholic all their lives, they had never heard the song before. In the early 1970s, when I moved back home with them, they used to love to sing that song together.

My dad developed cancer and died within six months. Mom lived five weeks longer, and then died of a broken heart. They had been married for over sixty years, and despite their advanced age, their passing was very painful for me.

One year later, I was visiting my sister in the Bahamas. On the flight over, I became very lonely for my parents. I prayed that I would be given a sign that they could contact me from the other side.

I was walking alone on the island three days later. It was a beautiful day, and I was enjoying the sun and cool breeze. I heard organ music coming from the woods. I walked to the music and saw a tiny church in the middle of nowhere. I entered the building and saw an elderly lady sitting at an organ. We smiled at each other and I sat down. She played a number of hymns. Then she looked at me and said "This hymn is for you." I was shocked when she started playing "The Doxology."

Mom and Dad's favorite hymn was played for me on a remote island in the Bahamas. I knew they were sending me a message.

Daniel Gulbin
Scranton, Pennsylvania
January 2001

Temper, Temper!

Following the death of my wife Florence, I decided to move to a smaller home and to rent the house we had occupied. In June 1977 my friend Betty Newhouse was helping me pack for the move.

I placed a small figurine in a box on the table; the box was about two-thirds full and the figurine lay about four inches from the top.

Several minutes later, as we continued to pack, I said to Betty, "I wonder what Florence would say if she knew I was renting this house to people of the _____ religion." This was a religion whose teachings were at odds with those of my wife's church.

Immediately after I asked this question, something hit the floor with a loud crash. It was the figurine. There was no way it could have fallen on its own from the box on the table because, as I said, it lay a good four inches below the top of the box.

As we continued to pack, I mused on the memory of Florence's quick temper. During our life together, if she had an object in her hand when something happened or was said to upset her, that object was given a quick pitch to the floor! Apparently her transition did not change her temper.

James M. O'Neill
McDonald, Ohio
July 1982

Father's Love and Blessing

Many years ago, at a time in my life when I was worried and depressed, I decided to make the 360-mile drive to visit my only aunt, Jennie Shaffer Hull, who lived in Falconer, a suburb of Jamestown, New York, to ask for advice. The only person I knew in that locality was Aunt Jennie.

After I had poured out my troubles, she asked if I would be willing to go to Lily Dale, the Spiritualist community, to get a reading from a medium. She had heard that many persons found help there. Although it was only thirteen miles from her home, she never had been there. There was no way anyone in Lily Dale could know anything of my life.

Today Lily Dale is widely known. It was not very large in August 1949 when we walked through the grounds wondering which cottage to stop at. Finally we selected a small white house. With shaking fingers I pressed the doorbell. A pleasant woman, about thirty years old, opened the door and asked me to step in.

All I wanted was an answer to something that was troubling me, so when I asked her if she would read for me and what she charged, her answer frightened me.

"I do not charge," she said, "but I will bring you messages from the dead and you can leave on the table whatever you think it was worth." I had not bargained for communication with the dead!

We were ushered into a small room, furnished only with a small table and three chairs. I sat across from the medium and my aunt took her place alongside me. The medium took both my hands in hers and closed her eyes. After a few seconds she started jerking. "Please be very quiet," she said. "The messages are not very loud."

First my grandfather Michael Shaffer came. He said he wanted me to know he was well and happy. Next came my grandmother Adeline. In life she was stern and outspoken, and what she said did not surprise me, for it was the sort of thing she would say: "You made your bed. Now lie in it."

Even though I recognized my grandmother's characteristic sharp tongue, still it did not convince me that the dead were speaking. The next message I received did.

Suddenly the medium jerked so hard I hardly could hold on to her hands. As she quieted she said, "Here is a very young, handsome man. He says he is your father and he has something he wants to give you. He could not give you this before, for he left the Earth before you came. His gift is a father's love and blessing."

I started to cry, for the fact of my father's death was absolutely correct. He had been a bookkeeper in his father's laundry and one day a heavy roll of paper fell from a high storage platform and struck him on the head. He regained consciousness only long enough to call my mother's name before he died.

My earthly troubles seemed to pale in the light of the monumental knowledge that the dead are very much alive. I was now ready to leave, but suddenly the medium turned to Aunt Jennie. Her first husband, John Shaffer, had been a bridge contractor. He went out early one morning to see that everything was in order for the men to start working on the bridge. He stepped on a loose plank, crashed to the pavement below, and died instantly. A year after his death my aunt married again, then began to wonder if she had broken faith with John. Should she have remained single?

We learned that afternoon that those above see us and know when we worry. John's message was: "Don't worry. You did exactly right in getting married again." Then Aunt Jennie started to cry and we left—but we made one mistake. When we stopped to put our money on the table we did not ask our reader's name. If she had business cards on the table we were too upset to notice. For fifteen years my husband Kenneth took me every year to Lily Dale, but we never did find her again.

Ruth N. Bixler
Halifax, Pennsylvania
January 1972

I Got the Message

On Saturday, January 23, 1965, three weeks after my father Frederick Kendall died, I had an experience that proved to me that life survives this plane of existence.

At noon that day I walked into my mother's house in Short Hills, New Jersey, and found my mother, Natalie Kendall, eating lunch in the living room as she watched a tennis match on television. I decided to let her be and to stroll around the house just to check things out.

I went upstairs and into my mother and father's bedroom; I opened the door to my father's walk-in closet. Totally lost in thought, I must have spent about five minutes looking at my father's things—shirts, suits, shoes.

By the time I shut the closet door, I was overcome by a deep sadness and the realization that I would never again hear my father's voice. He and I had been very close and I was going to miss him terribly. Tears came to my eyes. Instead of going back downstairs, I went into the hall bathroom to try to pull myself together.

I splashed my eyes and face with cold water. Instead of helping, this made me break down altogether. All the pent-up emotions I had tried so hard to control over the past few weeks came flooding out. No matter what I did, the sobbing continued. Since I was trying to comfort Mom, I certainly didn't want her to see me this way.

Finally, to snap myself out of my distress, I concocted a lie. "Why am I acting like this?" I said to myself. "Dad never really loved me anyway." As I spoke these words, I gained strength and control. At the same time, however, a feeling of guilt took hold of me.

Then, at that precise moment, an unspoken message sounded inside my mind. "Go downstairs," it said. "Your mother has something to tell you."

I knew that as soon as I opened the bathroom door my mother would call to me—and I knew exactly what she would tell me. To this day I can't explain it, but it was as if I had written a script and my mother acted it out.

I opened the door and stepped out into the hall to hear my mother call, "David, please come downstairs. I have something to tell you." As I entered the living room, she said, smiling nervously, "You're going to think I'm nuts but I just got a message from your father. He insists that I tell you that he loves you very much."

David A. Kendall
Madison, New Jersey
January 1984

Grandpa Called

My father-in-law William Rains had several light strokes. The last, in the fall of 1942, left him bedridden for three months before he died.

I had to care for him as if he were a child. He had to be watched all the time so that he would not harm himself or someone else.

Before I ever sat down to eat, I fed him first and sat with him while he smoked his pipe because otherwise he would hide it, still lit, under the covers.

Two weeks after he passed away, we were all seated at the dining table for the evening meal when suddenly I heard him call, "Girl, girl," as he was in the habit of doing whenever we would sit down to eat. I was always having to jump up to see what he needed.

I started to get up to go to him when it dawned on me that he was no longer there. I went on eating.

My nine-year-old son Glen glanced up at me and said, "Mom, Grandpa called you!" His eyes got big when he, too, remembered that Grandpa was no longer alive!

Both of us heard him plainly but we said nothing more.

Several times after that my husband and I were awakened during the night by the sound of Grandpa's rocking chair. But when we went to his room to check, there was no more rocking.

Leone L. Nash
Hughson, California
February 1987

The Blackboard Ghost

There it was in green and white—a message scrawled on the blackboard in the penmanship of an old, unsteady hand: "If G-d is with us, who can be against us." Above it, written in the same white chalk, was a Hebrew phrase in perfect, right-out-of-the-prayer-book print. The six of us looked in amazement at these words, not believing what we saw. This was impossible. No one had been in the house since the board had been erased earlier that day.

The third floor of Annette and Steve's one-hundred-year-old Victorian home had been converted into a playroom for their two young boys. Having just moved into the house a month before, the kids used the room to their greatest creative advantage. Its novelty had not worn off yet. The room was a conversation piece, and when guests arrived, it was the most popular feature on the house tour. Annette and I had been chatting with our husbands when my brother came downstairs. "I love the blackboard room," he said. "Who wrote in Hebrew on the wall?"

"What?" screamed Annette, as we all flew up the stairs to confirm the sight.

The appearance of this chalk message was unexplainable, but a strange coincidence put this handwriting in a more supernatural light.

Annette and Steve were trying to refurbish the home in the style of the 1940s. The man who lived at the house then was in his eighties and lived nearby. Annette invited him to dinner the following week, to pick his brain about how the house had looked and where to put several artifacts they had found lying around the property. Annette and Steve were very excited about learning about the house in its glory days. Apparently, this gentleman had been very attached to the residence and his life there.

Two days after the discovery of the unexplained hand-writing, Annette received some sad news. The former owner would not be coming to dinner after all. He had passed away two days before.

Did the former owner send a benevolent message about his life and feelings for this place? We'll never really know, but the timing gives us reason to suspect it.

Malerie Yolen-Cohen
Stamford, Connecticut
March 1999

I Learned a Lesson

I will never again leave a letter lying around in which I have spoken ill of the dead.

My father, Fred B. Wells, died on April 10, 1972, at St. Joseph's Hospital in Hillsboro, Wisconsin. He had been a brakeman on the Chicago & Northwestern Railway for forty years.

The next year I traveled to England, Wales, and Scotland, returning to my home in Janesville, Wisconsin, on September 28, 1973. On September 30, I started a letter to Dad's cousin Lois Jewell who lived in Anaheim, California, to tell her about my trip.

"There is such a chauvinistic attitude among the men over there," I wrote. "The deodorant ads are slanted for women only, and only the women have to pay to use public restrooms.

"And," I added, "I can sure see why Dad was such a stubborn Englishman. He came by it naturally, just like the men in that country now."

I found myself growing sleepy about midnight, so I left the letter, unfinished, on my desk and went to bed. I hadn't been asleep long when I was awakened by the sound of my father's footsteps in the hall—not the slow, shuffling, arthritic footsteps of his last few years but the quick, impatient sounds he had made as a young man. I turned on the bedside lamp and frantically shook my husband, Bill.

"Did you hear that? Someone is in the house." I couldn't bring myself to tell him I recognized the footsteps. But they had ceased abruptly when the light went on.

"You must have been dreaming," Bill said. "Turn off the light and go back to sleep."

I did—but again the footsteps started. I thought I would faint with fear as I snapped on the light. Bill had heard the sounds and now he got up. Grabbing a baseball bat from the hall closet he searched carefully through the whole house. He found nothing.

I was afraid to turn off the light. "It's Dad," I told Bill. "I know it is. I recognize the way he used to walk. A burglar wouldn't walk that fast. He'd walk more stealthily."

"Nonsense," Bill retorted. "Your father is dead—and there are no such things as ghosts."

I lay for at least an hour with the light on, my heart thumping. Things stayed quiet, so I finally turned off the light. Immediately the footsteps sounded—this time right alongside the bed. When another sinister sound began I flipped on the light. Horrified, I watched the dresser scarf on the bedside table flapping up and down on both sides, like a bird about to take wing! Almost hysterical now, I poked Bill and pointed to the flapping cloth. Seeing this, he did not protest when I left the light on for the rest of the night.

At daybreak I finished the letter and sealed it into an envelope. The presence never visited us before the night I wrote the letter, and has not returned since.

In my own mind I know Dad was disturbed by my comments about him. He was a good and loving father who never laid a hand on me, but he could be stern with anyone who talked about loved ones in a demeaning fashion. He had let me know I had said the wrong thing about him in my letter.

His ghostly visit taught me never to speak—or write—ill of the dead.

Eleanor Richardson
Janesville, Wisconsin
January 1983

When Dreams Become Reality

I was unprepared when my mother phoned me and told me that my childhood friend Donna had just passed away. My first reaction was that my mother had gotten it all wrong. But as she read the obituary I realized that it was true. The obituary, however, did not reveal the circumstances of Donna's death. I couldn't rest that night, so I wrote a letter to Donna's mother, telling her how sorry I was and asking if she could tell me how Donna died. While I wrote, I cried. I wept into the night.

In the early morning hours I fell asleep at last, and I dreamed of Donna. It was like no dream I had ever had; it had a different, ineffable quality. There was a heavy, palpable, gray mist surrounding the dreamscape, and Donna's image rose from the midst of it. She was sitting in a wheelchair. I paid no attention to the incongruity of seeing an able-bodied person in a wheelchair. "I knew my mother was wrong. I knew you were still here with us," I cried with sheer joy, running toward her.

She spoke to me, though her lips never moved. "No," she said and held up a hand so that I would come no closer. "I'm only here to tell you that there's no reason for you to grieve. If I had lived, this is what I would be."

I realized that her arms and legs were atrophied and that she looked nothing like she had in life, full of expressive beauty. Instead, she slumped in her chair, inert. "If I had lived, I would never have been the same," she said.

"But you're here," I argued.

"Yes," Donna assured me, "but only to help you understand that this was meant to be—that I have done what it was I needed to do. And now I have moved on. It was time and my body was broken." With these last words Donna's image faded. I awoke feeling drained, but somehow healed.

Weeks later, I received a response from Donna's mother. She reported that an aneurysm in Donna's brain had ruptured while giving birth to her daughter. Prior to the birth, no one had known about the aneurysm, including Donna. Then the words in the letter echoed what Donna had said in my dream: "If Donna had lived, she would have never been the same."

I put the letter down in awe. The dream had been a prophetic preamble to the letter. I knew that Donna had survived, but in a different world. While I had always believed that our consciousness survives death, the dream confirmed it for me. That was Donna's gift to me.

She did not visit my dreams again until years later. I had suffered from asthma for many years, but in 1993 I experienced such bad attacks that I felt they could become fatal. When they intensified, I felt physically and emotionally as though I might die. The feeling was so strong that I began scribbling letters of love and affection to my family, tucking them away in my nightstand. My intuition warned me that something ominous was about to happen.

At the height of my illness, Donna visited my dreams again. The same unmistakable feeling followed her sudden entrance. It was almost like having a television program interrupted for an important announcement. She stepped forward and came right to the point. "What do you want?" she asked, as though I had called her away from something important. "You are grieving again."

"I feel death all around me," I told her.

"Yes, there is death around you," Donna confirmed.

"Does it have to be?" I lamented. "When will it happen?"

"In July," she told me.

"But it's almost July," I cried.

"There will be a death in July," she reiterated.

I had the impression that she had given me foresight to steady and ground me, just as her appearance in my dream had helped me come to terms with her untimely death.

But it was not my own death that she heralded. On a Sunday morning in July, we received word that our twenty-four-year-old nephew, Ed, had died in an car accident.

I began to realize that my dream conveyed something more than prophecy: it communicated a deep spiritual message, confirming that all things in life go according to a divine plan. How could there be foreknowledge without some form of predestination in the cosmos? How could I be informed of something that hadn't happened yet if no plan existed?

I felt enlightened and transformed, the same way someone who has had a near-death experience might feel. I sensed in the deepest part of me the presence of a wondrous force that gave my life purpose and traveled with me as I made choices. The grandest gift of the discovery was that I could draw on that knowledge to find comfort and healing during times of turmoil and tragedy.

At last, I learned to pay attention to dreams, to appreciate their truth and wisdom. I found that dreams can guide us, help us find solutions, clarify choices, enhance our relationships, avoid and survive tragedy, and generally stay in tune with the people and events in our lives.

Lynn Jeffcott
Bettendorf, Iowa
April 1999

Big Ben Rang Again

Beginning in June 1966 I felt something terrible was going to happen to a member of my family, but I didn't know who. This feeling was shared by other members of the family—my husband Paul Kennedy, our twin daughters Elaine and Ellen, and our two sons Paul, Jr., and Andrew. Being a religious family, we prayed, but the feeling persisted.

A year later, on June 1, 1967, my beloved husband went fishing and accidentally drowned. Andy was in the air force en route to the Panama Canal Zone, but received a thirty-day leave for the funeral, as did Paul, Jr., who also was in the air force, stationed in Thailand. Ellen came from Houston, but Elaine, in Anchorage, Alaska, was ill and couldn't come.

After the funeral we talked of all the things we had done together and all the fun we had had, just as every family does after a death. Andy commented that "Big Ben" was still empty as it was when he left for the air force.

This was a family joke. Before enlisting in the service Andy had slept on the third floor of our big old house. He was hard to wake in the morning, so after Andy was asleep his father used to set a huge antique alarm clock in a pan by his bed.

Every morning Andy would remove the insides from Big Ben (as we called the clock) and hide them. Paul would search until he found the insides, put the clock back together and reset it for the next morning. And so the game had continued.

The morning Andy left for the air force, he removed Big Ben's insides and hid them as usual, but Paul had no reason to hunt for them. In fact, he seldom went up to the third floor at all after Andy left.

The morning after the funeral Andy came downstairs white-faced, holding Big Ben—now intact—in his hands. He was angry; he thought one of us had found the clock's works, replaced them, and set it as a joke. But not one of us had even been up to his third-floor room.

The incident really shook us when we realized this was Paul's way of letting us know he was still with us.

Matilda Kennedy Jumper
Marion, Indiana
April 1976

"Threading It Backwards"

When my mother, Consiglia Ciavarella, died in March 1964 in Chicago, my dad gave each of us children something from her belongings. Since my sister, Lillian Di Natale, was the seamstress, Dad gave her Mom's old Singer sewing machine.

On a quiet spring afternoon two months after Mom's death Lil opened the sewing machine—in her home in Cicero, Illinois—and began to do some sewing. But each time she started the thread would break. After this was repeated several times Lil sat back and said out loud, "Dear Mother, why is this happening? I've used the machine so many times in your home, but now that I'm using it in my house it won't work. Why?"

Then like a bolt of lightning a voice from down the hall behind her spoke clearly and loudly in Italian (which Mom used most of the time). Lil heard Mom's voice say, "You're threading it backwards."

Not thinking at that instant, Lil replied out loud, "Why, you're right. Thanks." Suddenly she realized it was our mother's voice and quickly made the sign of the cross.

Lil never mentioned her experience to anyone except me. She knew I was interested in the occult and wouldn't dismiss the voice as her imagination. Lil never has had any problem with the sewing machine since then.

Jeana Whitehouse
Virginia Beach, Virginia
July 1976

The Ghost, Ouija, and Grandpa

As a young child, I always slept with my door shut. Later, when I was a teenager, I believe I found out why.

I was fourteen years old, and I usually went to bed around nine o'clock. I shared my room with my older brother Jake. I awoke one morning at around five o'clock. As I looked up, I saw the white, glowing figure of a man coming into my bedroom. I looked on for a moment, then quickly shut my eyes tight and rolled onto my side. I was afraid, and hoped that he'd leave. As I lay there, I could feel his presence standing over me. I could actually hear heavy, shallow breathing coming from him. It seemed like hours passed before the alarm went off.

I mentioned nothing to my brother at first. I didn't really believe in ghosts, and neither did the rest of my family. Anticipating their reaction, I changed my story a little before I told them. I described the whole event as a dream. I must admit I was surprised to hear my mother say that she also had the same dream. She calls it a dream to this day, and says it still goes on.

My wife Sue has also had strange encounters. I told her of the ghost I had seen—the ghost who still haunts my parents' house. She decided to ask a Ouija board who the ghost was and what he wanted.

I watched for a couple of hours as she asked questions and wrote down answers. The board never identified the ghost, but to our shock, my Grandpa Jake came through, mentioning things that my wife couldn't have known. Jake died in 1984, long before Sue and I had met.

One thing startled us especially. Jake mentioned that I was going to carry on the family name. We looked at each other in awe, and she put the board away.

A month and a half later, we found out that Sue was pregnant—just as the board told us she was. There was no way either of us could know she was pregnant then. Nine months later, in October of 1998, our son Seth Mitchell was born. We've never tried the Ouija again, but I am now a firm believer in the afterlife.

Brian Slabe
Ilion, New York
March 2000

Afterlife Is Beautiful

In 1996, my husband passed away, and my oldest daughter took it really hard. She had never been much of a reader, but something told her to start reading books about life after death. She started going to bookstores and reading all those books. Once I asked her, "What are you looking for?"

She replied, "Mom, when I find it, I'll know."

A few months later, she asked me to come over because she had something she wanted me to hear. She told me she had started to read *The Dead Are Alive* by Harold Sherman. She didn't even finish the first chapter before she knew this was the one she was looking for.

The book tells you how to speak to the dead on a cassette player. The funny part is, a few weeks before my husband died, he had given her a cassette player. At the time she wondered why he would give her something like that—she had no use for it. She put the tape player away and forgot about it, until she read *The Dead Are Alive*.

She took out the tape player and decided to see what she could get on it, if anything. This would be a good time, since her husband was at work and the children were all in school. The house was quiet and she hit "Record" on the tape player. Not really expecting to get anything, she was in total shock when she played the tape back, only to hear her father speaking to her:

"Hi Chris, I'm happy. It's so beautiful here—you have no idea. Our life is just a whisper. Don't grieve for me, my daughter. I love you."

Since then, we have made many tapes, and we have heard from many deceased family members. Sometimes it's just a "Hi."

We accept this as a gift from God—one that we treasure.

Dolores Wienchutoni
Somerville, New Jersey
July 1999

A Call for Babe

My parents were inseparable, and when Father died Mother's grief caused her to go from 190 pounds to 114 pounds in weight. I was the youngest child and was Father's favorite, perhaps because I resembled Mother. His pet name for me— never used by others—was "Babe."

One night in May 1937, when Father had been dead for two years, I was waked by his voice calling, "Babe, Babe!"

"Yes, Father," I answered. I spoke so loudly that I woke my husband.

"You must have been dreaming of your father," he said. "I heard you mention him."

"I wasn't dreaming," I protested. "He called me and I know his voice."

A few minutes later I heard Father call me again and I answered. My husband suggested I sleep elsewhere so that he could get some rest, so I lay down on the davenport in the front room. I had just settled myself when I heard

Father call again. Then he spoke lovingly in his normal, familiar voice.

"Don't be afraid, Babe. In two weeks I'm coming for your mother. I came back to tell you so you won't be frightened when it happens."

In the morning I told my husband about the incident and he scoffed at my story. A week later Mother came to visit me, and the next morning, when I carried a breakfast tray to her room, I found her unconscious. I was frozen with panic but I remembered Father's words and grew calm.

Mother remained unconscious for over a week and the doctor told us that the end was near. I was standing at her bedside with my husband, his cousin, and his pastor when suddenly Mother opened her eyes. She looked directly at me, and said clearly, "Daughter, step aside. You are standing in front of your father."

We all looked around but saw nothing. The pastor took her hand and said gently, "Mr. Saunders isn't here, my dear."

"Yes, he is," she said firmly. "He has come to take me home, to our house where we lived for thirty-five years."

Glancing at me she continued, "You had better pack my things and stop standing in front of your father."

I moved obediently.

"My," she sighed, smiling her old, gay smile, "how wonderful my Genie looks. I'd be glad to stay with you," she apologized to me, "but I'd rather go home. We'll go soon now."

A half hour later she died.

At Mother's funeral service, the minister told of this incident and said, "I am no Spiritualist, but I really believe Mr. Saunders came and took his beloved wife home."

My husband pressed my hand to tell me he believed it too.

Alice S. Napier
Modesto, California
July 1955

Hurry with the Headstone

My mother died on October 31, 1997. Her death was especially hard for me because we had grown so close during her last year. I wasn't there when she died, and this fact always stayed with me.

I had the task of picking out her tombstone. I wanted something nice, so I ordered a stone with flower etchings on it. They told me that this might take a bit longer due to all the extra etching.

My husband Miles often sleeps in our spare bedroom, where I had set up Mother's bed. Miles is one of those people who never remembers his dreams. One day in November, he came into our room and announced that he had just talked to my mother. This didn't upset him; he was more in a state of awe.

Miles said that Mother told him to tell me to get the headstone on her grave because she was "tired of telling folks who I am." She mentioned the flowers that were being etched on her stone. (I hadn't told Miles about that because it cost so much.)

I knew in my heart that Mother talked to Miles that morning. No one else had known about the flowers, and her quotations sounded exactly like what she would have said to me.

Of course, I immediately had the headstone job rushed, so that Mom wouldn't have to "tell folks" who she was.

Kathryn A. Brooks
Atlanta, Texas
September 1999

Electronic Visits

Two months after my husband's unexpected death in 1992, his spirit came to visit. I had fallen asleep in bed when my stereo woke me up, playing full blast. It startled me, but I didn't think much of it. I assumed I had left it on accidentally. Then I remembered that it had not been on the night before.

The next day I mentioned this incident to my friend.

"Eleanor," she said, "Paul came to visit last night."

My friend had been awakened on her sofa by her dog barking at her door. She turned to see what the dog was upset about and saw Paul standing by the door in white clothing. She sat up, rubbed her eyes, and said his name, but he was gone.

On Paul's birthday in 1997, my daughter Katie called to say she needed a ride home. When I went to the car, I had a message on my cell phone. That was strange, because my daughter was the only one who ever called me on it. When I retrieved the message, I was shocked to find that the entire conversation that I had had with my daughter on my home phone was recorded on my cell phone voice mail. I have been told that this is impossible.

Paul's favorite time of the year was the holidays. That same year we were again packing for Christmas vacation. Katie had a Tamagotchi doll, which were all the rage a few years back. The battery had run dead and she had not played with it for months. While she was packing, it began beeping. She looked at it and its little display window read, "Hi Katie." Since there is no way to type anything into the toy, I knew that it was Paul. After a while, the screen went blank. This happened again on Christmas Day.

Since Paul was quite a bit older than me, he always joked about coming back to visit if he died. I now know he meant it. It has been more than a year since his last visit. I miss him, but it was time for his spirit to move on.

Eleanor Ahlstrand
Sacramento, California
October 1999

A Gift of Reassurance

I was spending the weekend with my dear friend Jackie. Sadly, two weeks earlier she had buried a friend from her cancer support group. At the end, this poor young woman—suffering so with pain, worried over the teenage daughter she was leaving behind, and very frightened—naturally took out some of her fear and frustration on those around her.

Jackie spoke of her uncertainty that their relationship was intact at the end. Did her friend forgive her for impatience Jackie might have shown, in response to the dying woman's demands and sharp words? As Jackie perceived it, their long friendship had ended badly—and unresolved. She was tormenting herself with this analysis.

My angels, whom I hold close and their counsel dear, popped the answer into my head, one I personally would not have been so bold to say by myself. I suggested to Jackie that soon after death, sometimes one can call out to a soul for reassurance, resolution—perhaps a sign. There are hundreds of such documented, true accounts.

We pleaded with the woman's spirit to show us some sign that she understood, and was happy and free of human frailties and faults; that all was forgiven and restored. With this, we continued with our relaxed evening of television and talk of other things, laughing at ourselves to think anything would actually happen, and in any case, having no clue what to expect.

Then, quite suddenly, a paper that had been well secured to the refrigerator for a long time flew off, did several curls in the air, and came to lay on the carpet in the center of the room. We didn't think much about it, and replaced the paper, checking for drafts or vents, but finding nothing.

Then, a nearby floor lamp began to flicker. Jackie inspected the wire, bulb, wall switch, and base. We considered the lack of road traffic or inclement weather. She insisted this had never before occurred. I joked that maybe her friend on the other side was truly attempting to give a signal. We were spooked, but thought we were simply missing a natural phenomenon.

Later, the light flickered again, this time staying off longer at each interval. Now, we were calling her friend's name aloud and welcoming her visit and response.

Finally, the strangest, most convincing thing of all occurred. Jackie had a small dish of candy sitting back on a cupboard across the room. By now, we were quite alert, not distracted by the television. I was thinking only of how wonderful it was to be blessed by signs which might come to comfort my friend. We watched in amazed silence as a chocolate candy kiss rose from the dish, floated horizontally across several feet of airspace, and tumbled to an abrupt landing at Jackie's feet.

We sat in utter shock, neither of us able to believe our very sober eyes, and too frightened to touch the candy. I was covered in goose bumps and my hair stood on end. Several moments passed before either of us could speak, but when we did, it was in a fast-paced, nervous chatter. We recognized that we had, in fact, been contacted.

Later, we thanked the spirit for her grace and all that it took to convince us. Jackie expressed, through joyous facial features and relaxed shoulder muscles, that she believed her friend was all right, forgave her (as if that were necessary), and loved Jackie for caring for her until the end of her earthly life. We are now certain there is another existence— a kinder, gentler life beyond this one, where a Supreme

Being occasionally allows for the gift of reassurance and hope.

M. Maureen McNulty
Columbus, Indiana
April 2000

The Phoning Nun

On December 1 of each year, I begin to write my Christmas cards. On December 1, 1998, I paged through my Christmas data book, checking the list of who sent a card the year before. On the last page is the name of the nun who taught me in commercial class. After graduation I kept in touch with her, and every year I mailed her a card with a ten-dollar bill.

Sister Rita had been sent to a home for retired nuns, but I managed to visit her often. Every letter she sent urged me forward in my work. She was my inspiration, and I loved her and looked for her guidance.

Sister Rita came to me in a dream last year to let me know she was going to Heaven. It was strange to see her rising up into the heavens on an elevator. Right after the dream, I received a phone call that she had passed away on February 24, 1998.

Now, as I cherished her memory, I felt very sad, wishing I could still mail her a Christmas card or make contact.

I was alone when the telephone rang at exactly 8:00 P.M. I answered with a "Hello" and the most beautiful voice responded, "Hello." Immediately I was aware that the voice belonged to someone I loved. The voice was soft and musical and asked, "Lillian?"

"Speaking," I answered.

"How are you?"

"Fine," I answered, trying to identify the voice.

"What are you doing?"

"Writing Christmas cards," I said, and following that I asked, "And to whom am I speaking?"

The voice lovingly responded, "This is Sister Rita from the Franciscan Order."

Now there was a lull—no dial tone, just stone silence. I held the phone in mid-air for several minutes, stunned. I hung up, shaking in disbelief.

Still in shock, I went to my Christmas data book and marked an X in the space reserved for incoming cards—in the "received" column next to Sister's name.

Yes, Sister sent me a most beautiful greeting with that call. I feel certain that call came from Heaven, for I'm sure that is where she is.

Lillian E. Burton
River Grove, Illinois
June 1999

Apparitions
Return Visits by the Departed

Among the "survival" stories in *FATE*'s archives, some of the most dramatic are among the hundreds in which a deceased person is reported to have visited a friend or family member after death. The visitor may bring a message of encouragement or concern to the witness, or simply offer hope and assurance by his or her presence.

The classic example of this type of report in our culture is that of Jesus's Easter return to his followers. But such reports are found in all cultures, and continue to the present day.

Moral Support

My father had been dead for a couple of years when my mother was asked to do a reading for a prayer service at our church. It would be the first time she read to a group larger than the circle of her own children.

My mother was understandably nervous, and I sat in the front pew to give her all the moral support I could. I knew she would do well, but I asked for a little divine intervention anyway.

The prayer service was small and only the lights in the front section were fully lit. As my mother approached the pulpit, I felt a chill come over me. I was compelled to look at our usual seat in the left transept. I sat in awe of the vision before me. It was the figure of my father, gliding down the aisle toward the front pew. He was wearing the brown suit in which he had been buried. I shook my head and rubbed my eyes, thinking it was only my imagination, but when I looked again he was still there.

My mother began her reading, unaware of my distraction. After finishing, she returned to her seat beside the pulpit. I looked back to where I had seen my father's image. He was gone. The chill I had felt throughout the reading was replaced by a warmth, as if someone were hugging me.

Later, I mentioned this to my mother. Although she had not seen or felt anything while at the lectern, she did not doubt me. I have always been sensitive that way. She did, however, admit to feeling a warm hug when she stepped away from the microphone.

In the years since my father's passing, there have been many occasions when we have both felt Dad's presence at home, as if he were helping us with some task that he had always been better at. However, I have not seen his image since that incident in the church.

Elizabeth M. Dumont
Bristol, Connecticut
February 1999

A Comfort?

I was thirteen when my grandmother, Minnie McClendon, died in 1952. I loved her dearly and was grief-stricken by her sudden death. My parents, Donald and Jessie McClendon, and I traveled to Moran, Texas, for the funeral. While there I sometimes thought I heard my grandmother's voice calling me from the kitchen in her familiar way, "Honey, come on out in the kitchen with me." Each time I almost answered before remembering she was dead. Then I would break into sobs.

Through some confusion, I didn't get to sit with my parents next to Grandmother's casket at the funeral, and I resented this.

The following day we returned home to Eastland, Texas. I was very tired. That night in bed I was about to drop off to sleep, but when I rolled over on my side facing the window I bolted wide awake. There stood Grandmother beside my bed in her light-blue funeral gown, her long hair hanging loosely about her shoulders. I was so startled I hid my face. When I looked again she was gone.

Now, years later, I often wonder if Grandmother came to comfort me because of my grief and disappointment at not getting to sit next to her casket.

Beverly Hutcheson
Tijeras, New Mexico
April 1974

The Shining Form

In 1962 my father Glenn Henderson died of leukemia in a small hospital in Pecos, Texas. In his last hours of life my mother and I reassured him of our love.

While in a coma, he had been calling my mother's name for over three hours. When he fell silent and the doctor pronounced him dead, it was almost a relief. The doctor was accompanied by a nurse and an assistant. Father's bed had been raised to a sitting position so that he could breathe more easily. The nurse later returned the bed to the prone position.

I told her that I had heard music the entire time. She assured me that no music was playing at that hour, which was shortly after three o'clock in the morning. My mother slumped into my arms as we sat on a settee nearby.

Suddenly the nurse said to the doctor, "Do you see it?"

We looked up and saw a small figure, above my father's prone body, shining as though wrapped in silver foil. It was in a sitting position, with knees bent and arms outstretched. It was joined to my father's body by a silver cord.

We could see the window across from the bed through the rising form. All was gone in less than a minute.

While not a religious man, my father was a spiritual one. Of course, what Mother and I saw could be explained as an illusion due to our emotional states, but a doctor and two nurses also witnessed the event. They certainly were removed from this happening emotionally, having been in contact with my father for less than twenty-four hours.

The nurse later said it was the second time she had witnessed such an event. It has been a great comfort to Mother and me through all the following years. The experience confirmed our belief that we live on after death. My father was a strong and loving man who would give us proof of that if he could.

Robert C. Henderson
Land O'Lakes, Florida
March 1989

The Comeback

During my senior year in college my father Charles Sauer died on his way home from his midnight-to-eight job. His fatal heart attack in December 1971 did not really surprise my mother Elizabeth and me. Dad had refused to see any doctor after our family physician had warned him five years earlier that his days were numbered if he persisted in chain-smoking and drinking his daily quart or two of beer.

Once the first frenzied days of bereavement had passed, my mother returned to work and I to school. We grappled with feelings of grief and loss but we did not cling to this tragedy; we went on with our lives.

Then, in March 1972, I awakened a few hours before dawn in terror, shivering uncontrollably, my heart pounding. Although I was in the dark I knew that someone was standing near my bed. I could feel a presence. Just as suddenly as I realized a man was in the room, I knew it was my father.

I chided myself. *Absurd*, I thought, *the dead make house calls only in Halloween stories.* With all the courage I could summon, I peeked from under my down comforter and switched on the night-light. No one was in the room.

I dismissed the incident as a subconscious rebellion against the stoicism with which I had accepted my father's death. The experience proved I was human after all.

As I dressed the next morning, I resolved not to say anything to my mother. Even if I related the incident in a joking manner, I feared it would upset her. Yet it had been so vivid that I had to struggle to resist blurting out the tale at breakfast. I need not have concerned myself.

"Don't laugh," Mother said, "but the strangest thing happened to me last night. I woke up about 3:00 A.M. and could have sworn your father was standing beside my bed. When I finally found the courage to turn on the light, he wasn't there." As if trying to convince herself, she continued, "Of course he wasn't. How silly to let my nerves shake me up so!"

I believe my father did visit us both that night. He had not had an opportunity to say farewell. I think he came back to do just that.

Eileen Sauer
Richmond Hill, New York
October 1984

Father Martin's Message

On a crisp October morning in 1964 we received word of the death in a highway accident of a young friend, Father Martin. He had been assistant to the pastor at a church near our home in Richmond Heights, Missouri. He had fallen asleep at the wheel of his car and crashed head-on into a huge tractor-trailer rig. He was dead when the highway patrolmen arrived.

His body was brought back to his church where he lay in state for several days while stricken parishioners filed past the casket to pay their final homage. My family and I were among the mourners. Although I am not a Catholic, Father Martin had been a good friend with whom I had spent many pleasant hours discussing the Bible, theology, and the hereafter. We often discussed whether the Jewish people in Biblical times had believed in life after death, or if this precept is peculiar to Christian teachings.

Early in the afternoon before his funeral on November 8, 1964, we visited the church once more. As I knelt before the casket I wondered: Had Father now learned the answers to all the questions we had been asking?

About 3:15 that afternoon, having returned from a shopping trip, I started downstairs to the laundry room. Suddenly and inexplicably I felt someone or something close behind me. An ice-cold surge of terror paralyzed my body. I couldn't move! All I could see was a mist, but the mist formed a human outline. It was Father Martin—his distinctive face, light hair, and slim form.

Although it seemed longer, the experience lasted little more than a few moments. The mist dissolved and my paralysis lifted.

Now, years later, I am certain of what happened that autumn afternoon, and I know what it meant. Father Martin and I had talked many times of ghostly visitations during the first days after death. In a most convincing manner he had given me definite proof of survival beyond physical death.

Beverly C. Jaegers
Richmond Heights, Missouri
July 1971

Grandfather's Cane

When I was growing up, my grandfather, Victor White, lived in the small town of Marlin, Texas, ten miles from our home in Reagan. He died from complications of a stroke when I was twelve years old. He had been partially para-lyzed and walked with a cane.

About one week after his death in May 1953, I was sitting on the couch in our living room when I heard footsteps coming up the sidewalk. My grandfather had walked in a characteristic way; he would take a step and then drag the other foot. These were the exact sounds that I heard as I sat on the couch, although I didn't realize that I was hearing Grandfather's footsteps. Knowing that beggars would occasionally come to the house asking for food, I thought at first it was one of them.

When I went outside to look, I saw no footprints in the dirt that covered part of the sidewalk—but leaning against the steps of the porch was my grandfather's walking cane.

To this day no one knows how that cane made its way to our house—ten miles from Marlin to Reagan.

Jill Rapp
Bryan, Texas
August 1987

The Visitor

My husband spent the last two months of his life in a private room in the Kelowna Hospital in Kelowna, British Columbia. It was late 1965 and he was dying of cancer. I spent all my days at his bedside, leaving only once in a while to pick up our mail or get books from the library.

One afternoon when I returned after an absence of about two hours he greeted me excitedly, "Guess who came to visit while you were gone! Lou Gunn!"

That's odd, I thought. *Lou lives in Edmonton and doesn't even know my husband is ill.* Lou had been his closest friend during the many years we had lived in Edmonton.

"How did he know you were in the hospital?" I asked.

"I don't know; he just did," came the vague answer.

I looked closely to see if my husband had been influenced by some drug. His eyes looked perfectly normal and clear.

"Lou had a very serious heart attack," my husband continued. "On November 2 out of the blue he was stricken with a coronary thrombosis."

November 2! This was November 28. If Lou had sustained a serious coronary only twenty-six days ago, he could not possibly have traveled the distance to Kelowna.

"Are you sure Lou was here? Maybe you went to sleep and dreamed while I was gone."

My husband, now indignant, replied, "I haven't slept one minute. Lou was here and he talked to me. Why don't you ask the nurse? She'll know."

All visitors had to have the nurse's permission to enter my husband's room. I went to the desk and asked if he had had any visitors. The answer was no. Had he been given any medication? Nothing whatsoever for the past three days.

Back in his room I told him that he had dreamed Lou's visit. He became quite angry and insisted it was not a dream.

Four weeks later I received a letter from Lou's wife telling me that his heart attack on November 2, 1965, had been fatal. He died within an hour of the attack. But my husband insisted he saw Lou twenty-six days later.

Anna Irvine
Kelowna, British Columbia, Canada
September 1967

Meeting after Death

My son Richard, who had an intense interest in the psychic world, died of a massive stroke on April 3, 1985, and was buried one week later. Normally this ends the story of a dead person.

But this story really starts twenty months later on the evening of December 3, 1986. Frank Brown (pseudonym), a friend and childhood playmate of my son's, called from Downey, California, to say he was planning to visit a relative near El Paso, Texas, and wondered if he could visit me as well. He said he had gotten my phone number from Richard—in the month of December 1985!

I said that was impossible, that Richard had died almost two years earlier. Frank insisted he met Richard in Downey in December 1985 and they went to a small café. They talked for about an hour, during which Richard gave Frank accurate information about me, my phone number, and Richard's last address. Frank was certain about the date of the meeting.

I checked the address that Richard had given Frank. It was the same as the last one I had for Richard before he died; the phone number he used there was also accurate.

Frank didn't know Richard was dead until I told him so.

Cosette Willoughby
Fairacre, New Mexico
August 1987

He Kissed My Hand

My husband Aaron Elek and his parents were Hungarian by birth. My in-laws were sentimental and emotional people, especially my father-in-law Aron Elek, an Old World gentleman to whom hand-kissing was second nature. After a long illness he died in 1967, and my mother-in-law followed him within three months.

Our son Emery was born late in my in-laws' life and was very special to them. Because our home in Bay City, Michigan, was so distant from a church of their faith Emery never was baptized during their lifetimes. But early in 1972 we finally put our minds to it and made the arrangements for his baptism.

On Sunday, February 13, 1972, we drove three hundred miles to Cleveland, Ohio, to the Hungarian Reformed Church my husband had attended during his teens. The minister of the church, who coincidentally bore the same name as my husband, Aaron Elek, was delighted to perform the ceremony for us.

We arrived at the church shortly before the service. My husband was ushered immediately into the pastor's office. I followed slightly behind. Several people greeted us cordially as welcome strangers although most of them spoke only Hungarian and I do not know the language. One gentleman in particular came right up to me. He was just under average height and wore the traditional mustache of elderly Hungarian men. He smiled warmly as he reached for my hand. I thought he wanted to shake hands but he lifted my hand and kissed it with some emotion.

Just then my husband called me to the office to complete filling out papers for the baptism. When we finished and left the office I looked for the man who had greeted me so warmly in order to introduce my husband. But the man was nowhere in sight. *He might be an usher*, I decided. I would look for him during the service.

But as the service progressed I saw no sign of the man. I described him to friends who were members of the church but they could not identify him from my description.

After the service, my curiosity aroused, I asked my husband and his friends to help me search for the elusive gentleman. But the elderly Hungarian was nowhere to be found.

When I described the man again my husband observed that my description fit only one person—his father. That brought me to a halt, for it was true. I had seen my father-in-law frequently during his long illness, but it had been several years since I had seen him up and about. Both the appearance and the mannerisms of the unidentified man exactly matched those of my deceased father-in-law.

I feel that Aron Elek came back to show me that he was pleased we finally had Emery baptized after such a long delay.

Patricia Elek
Bay City, Michigan
June 1973

My Friend Maria

I attended the University of the Americas in Mexico City during the 1967–68 school year. I was a junior, majoring in philosophy. Logic and dialectic were the tools with which I proved and examined all statements and beliefs. I believed man's power—indeed, his very humanity—revolved around his ability to reason. Accordingly, I scorned anything that smacked of the "irrational," including religious experiences of an extraordinary nature, psychic phenomena, and out-of-body experiences.

During the Christmas vacation of 1967 some friends and I rented a villa in the seaside town of Playa Azúl. This Pacific Ocean town is approximately two hundred miles north of Acapulco. Our live-in maid and cook was a woman named Maria Sanchez, a charming, although quiet and serious woman of about fifty-five years.

Because of a severe sunburn I spent most of the vacation relaxing in the villa and I got to know Maria rather well.

Although she had little formal schooling, she possessed a quick wit and keen sense of observation. Our long talks ranged freely from topic to topic. She was deeply religious and told me many stories of miracles and visions. I dismissed these tales as local folklore. She firmly maintained that she herself had seen visions. I laughed and told her she had an overactive imagination.

After I returned to the United States I occasionally wrote Maria a short letter or postcard. She answered regularly with long, carefully written letters.

In 1970 I was drafted into the army and sent to Vietnam. My faith in reason was shattered by the hell I found there. *This is what "rational" men do?* I asked myself.

In September 1970 I was wounded and sent to the regimental hospital. I was in a state of deep depression and knew that I would never survive my tour of duty. I was certain I would be killed or crippled, or that I would "freak out."

One night I had the most vivid dream of my life. I was sitting on a beach in my uniform with my rifle by my side. Maria sat by me silently and stroked my head. Her cool, soothing palm on my forehead filled me with a wonderful peace.

I awoke the next morning feeling calm and somehow confident that everything would turn out for the best. I immediately sat down and wrote Maria a letter.

I returned to duty strangely purged of my depression. In late December I received a letter from Maria's daughter Graciela Moisés. She apologized for not writing sooner.

Her mother, she told me, had died in September. She said that her mother had been very fond of me and often had spoken of me.

I still think about Maria often. I am certain that our friendship transcended those barriers of time and space in a manner that cannot be explained logically or "rationally."

Francis E. Kazemek
Urbana, Illinois
June 1976

Diane

I am a fourteen-year-old who has had several supernatural experiences. This one has to do with ESP, a psychic trait that has been passed from mother to daughter in our family for generations.

One night four years ago I went to bed. I fell asleep and soon began to dream. In the dream my mother and I were sitting around the kitchen table. The kitchen was dimly lit. Outside it was dark. In front of me, hovering two feet above the floor, was the transparent figure of a girl in her late teens. She wore a short-sleeved white blouse and a calf-length red skirt. Her dark brown hair was loose and flowing and there was a smile on her pale face. She scared me. I sat and stared. My mother, seeing that I was frightened, touched my shoulder and said, "Don't worry, she won't hurt you. She's my friend."

I woke up at 10:40 P.M., so I went back to sleep. The next morning I told my mother about the dream. She was amazed when I described what the girl looked like. At the same time that I had my dream she had been thinking about her friend Diane and she couldn't sleep.

Diane was my mother's best friend growing up, and had died at age nineteen. I had described Diane exactly.

Carly Pazakis
West Yarmouth, Massachusetts
December 1994

John Returned

My brother John Stuart Locke, aged nineteen, died on April 19, 1966, at Lincoln College in Lincoln, Illinois, when a train hit him at a crossing. I heard about it on the radio in the biology lab at Evanston Township High School in Mr. Martin's class, where I was a fifteen-year-old freshman.

My father came to pick me and my sister up. We went down to Lincoln to get John's things. My grandparents lived in Pontiac and we met them there. John was buried in Taylorville, Illinois, the family's old hometown. It was hard for all of us.

A short time later, at home, I heard the doorbell ring and went to answer it. It was John. Strangely, when I saw him, I forgot he was dead. I thought he had come home from college. He came in the door. I was going to go to the kitchen to get my parents (who had not heard the doorbell,

I learned later) but John said he couldn't stay long. He gave me a hug, said goodbye, and went out the door. I closed it, then opened it again to see him leave—but he wasn't there.

I ran to the kitchen to tell my parents.

Richard Locke, Jr.
Evanston, Illinois
September 1985

Dad's Visit

My husband Joe and I have had several paranormal experiences during our lives, individually before we met and since our marriage thirty-one years ago. We are down-to-earth, commonsense people not given to flights of fancy. Our experiences are accepted as important facets of our lives and sometimes, the lesson to be learned from an encounter is not always clear at the moment it happens. This is an account of one experience I had.

It was a chilly Monday night in the fall and my husband was watching a football game on a TV set in our bedroom, while I sat in the living room watching a movie on another set. It was about 9:30 P.M. I had been watching a movie and dozed off, which I was prone to do occasionally. Upon waking, I saw it was a little after ten o'clock. Having missed about thirty minutes of the movie I had planned to see, I decided to go to bed to read.

I went into the bathroom and began removing my makeup and brushing my teeth. While bending over the sink, I had an uncontrollable urge to look into our living room, where I had just been sitting ten or fifteen minutes earlier. I had heard no noise, nor had I any reason to glance down the hall, except this almost uncontrollable need to look to my left. As I looked down our seven-foot hall to the living room, I saw a man walking from our living room into our kitchen. He was wearing a short-sleeved white shirt with dark trousers, and his head was bent slightly forward. I saw only the side view of the man.

Why would Joe change his clothes this late in the evening? I thought. My husband had been dressed in a red shirt and blue jeans. I then walked to the bedroom, where I had last seen my husband sitting and, behold—there he sat in a red shirt and jeans. I immediately jumped into the bedroom and sat on the edge of the bed.

Joe said "What's the matter, you look like you've seen a ghost."

I replied, "I just saw a man walk from the living room into the kitchen."

Joe jumped up from the chair and ran to the living room and kitchen to confront the intruder. I followed closely on his heels and said, "It's all right—I know who it was."

Joe turned to me and said, "What do you mean?"

"It was Les," I answered.

My father, a former college and professional football player, had owned a family sports tavern in Grand Island, Nebraska. His work uniform was always a short-sleeved white shirt and dark trousers. A tall man at six feet, four inches, he often walked with his head bent forward—more a habit of dealing with his bifocals than his height.

I walked into the kitchen and looked, but no one was there. I looked around the entire kitchen, including upward toward the ceiling and softly whispered, "I'm glad you're here watching over me and taking care of us. I know we didn't always see eye-to-eye, but I always knew you loved me and hope you knew how much I loved you—we just had trouble saying the words to each other. I'm happy to see you."

I then returned to my bedtime preparations. The day ended with special thoughts of my father, Les McDonald, who had died of a heart attack on July 26, 1971, some twenty-five years earlier. I am happy, comforted, and secure in the knowledge that my father is watching over our family. As in life, he remains a man who does not speak the words of love, but he bestowed a rare gift to me of glimpsing him for a moment, thus reinforcing that he and mother are always close at hand, watching over us and guiding us through life.

The knowledge that my father was watching over me gave me untold strength during painful times when I felt very alone in my battle.

Linda McDonald Williams
Knightdale, North Carolina
January 2000

My Dead Return

What I am about to relate is not a product of belief. It is a product of experience. I present it to you as pure unadulterated fact.

My first son Tommy was twenty-three days old when my father Thomas Orkney was killed. He fell from a truck in Puget Sound Naval Shipyard in Bremerton, Washington, on May 11, 1956, and was instantly killed.

Six months later, when my husband Milan Pecka was working the 12:00 to 8:00 A.M. shift, I was awakened at three o'clock one morning by my infant son's crying. Assuming he was wet or hungry, I arose and stumbled toward the baby's crib across the room from my bed. To my amazement I saw that the old-fashioned, black, enameled, wooden rocking chair at the foot of my bed was rocking to and fro. I wondered if we were experiencing a minor earth tremor.

As I approached the crib I distinctly heard my father's voice say, "Don't pick him up, Barbara, you'll only spoil him. He's neither wet nor hungry. He's teething and that makes him fussy. Let him cry a little and he'll go back to sleep."

This scared the daylights out of me. In one leap I was back in my bed with the covers over my head. Was I losing my mind? But that was my father's voice—as clear and normal as if he were physically alive and in the room with me.

In the years that followed I had two more children, Charlie and Therese, and then on November 22, 1967, my husband Milan Pecka died. In March 1968 I remarried and then had, in addition to my own three children, three foster children, Gary Rose and Connie and Lori Sidwaski.

We rented an old farmhouse on the highway between Raymond and Pe Ell, Washington. The house had not been occupied for fifteen years when we moved in, and we spent time fixing it and putting in a garden. One evening when the garden had been in about six weeks, the children and I were home alone; my husband was working the swing shift. At about nine o'clock Gary, fifteen, went into the darkness of the kitchen for a drink of water.

"Mom, come quick! Hurry!" I heard him call.

I put down my knitting and went to where Gary stood transfixed by something he saw outside the window. We had a lot of wildlife around the old farmhouse and I assumed he was watching a coyote, a deer, an elk, or something of the kind.

"Look, Mom," he whispered, "out there by the garden."

As I peered out I could see the moon shining through the trees in the orchard. And right at the end of the new garden stood the form of a man, wearing a robe. It appeared translucent in the moonlight.

"That's just my dad, Gary, come to see how the garden's growing," I said. The apparition immediately disappeared and as I turned to leave the kitchen I wondered why I had said that.

For several months following that incident the other five children made it a practice to get out of bed after dark and traipse down to the kitchen for a drink of water, hoping to get a glimpse of "Grandpa" in the garden, but he never returned.

The following year we bought a thirty-seven-acre farm closer to the town of Raymond where my husband worked. One July evening in 1969 after my husband had gone to work and all the chores were done I was playing the game "ESP" with the children. My younger son Charlie suddenly rose from the table and walked to the center of the living room. After standing there for a few seconds, he asked, "Mom, where's Grandpa?"

I explained for the umpteenth time that his grandpa had died before he was born and, as far as I knew, was in heaven.

"But you say he'll be with us always," he retorted. "Could he be right here in the room with us?"

"I really don't know, son," I replied. "I suppose he could."

"How would I know if he was here in the room?"

Becoming impatient with his line of questions, I retorted, "Well, Charlie, I suppose you could ask him if he is here."

And he did. Gathering all the courage he could muster, eight-year-old Charlie, hands on hips, asked, "Grandpa, are you in this room with us?"

Nothing happened, except a chill seemed to pass over us.

"Grandpa," Charlie demanded, "if you're in this room with us I want you to prove it. Now!"

At the opposite end of the living room was a plate glass window, eight feet wide and four feet high. I had hung curtains, with a ruffle across the top, at the window. As soon as

Charlie had uttered his challenge the ruffle began to quiver. It quivered progressively across the window from left to right.

Instantaneously there were five children in my lap. The card table lay on its side, having been knocked over in the melee. All six of us witnessed the answer Charlie's grandpa gave him. He was there!

I do not know what to expect in the future. But I do know there is life beyond the end of life here on earth, because I have had experiences that prove it to me. And I even have five witnesses to one of these experiences.

Barbara L. Pecka
Vancouver, Washington
April 1984

The Third Daughter

In January 1932, when the Depression was at its worst, I was a nurse doing "private duty," which in those days meant working twelve to twenty hours at a stretch. People rarely went into hospitals when they were ill at that time, as hospital insurance was a rare commodity. When illness occurred a nurse was called into the home.

In this case it was the mother who was ill. The rest of the family included her husband and two unmarried daughters, each well past forty years of age. The family was wealthy. The husband had brought his bride to this same home fifty-two years before. The place had been an orange ranch then running from Figueroa Street to Western Avenue. It is now part of southwest Los Angeles. In the early '30s the home was old but still lovely, with all the elegance of the bygone days.

Since my shift was from seven at night to seven in the morning, I was familiar with the many creaks and squeaks in the place. When they retired for the night the family always wanted to be reassured that I would call them if any change occurred in the patient's condition. None of them ever looked in on us during the night, so complete was their confidence in me.

This particular night I had made my patient comfortable and then settled myself in a large chair, behind which was a floor lamp. Over this lamp I draped a blanket. The light shone over my shoulder and onto my book only.

As I sat reading I heard someone come down the hall. She walked softly into the bedroom and came to stand at the foot of the mother's bed, resting both hands on the foot-rail. She was turned away from where I sat with my book and the room was only dimly lit. I did not see her face but I could see she was clad in a white flannel nightgown. It was old-fashioned with a yoke and a ruffle around the neck. The sleeves were long, with ruffles at the wrists. She was barefoot.

I was not startled that one of the daughters would check on her mother during the night, although no one ever had done so before. Since it was January I felt she should put on slippers and a robe. I started to tell her this but as soon as I spoke there was no longer anyone there.

The figure had seemed solid enough. I never once thought that it was not one of the living daughters until the figure vanished.

Later, I managed to learn in a roundabout way that none of the family had left their beds during the night. But I never mentioned this experience to any member of the family.

Weeks later I visited a friend whose landlady was another old-time resident of the neighborhood who knew this family. When I finished telling of my experience this elderly woman said, "There was a third daughter who died in her early twenties. Probably it was she who came to take her mother."

This could have been the case, for at dawn my patient slipped away from this world. Her unknown visitor had come at one o'clock that same morning.

Vivian F. Roberts, R.N.
Bell, California
July 1964

A Walk in the Park

Eight years ago my newlywed husband and I were enjoying exploring the quaintness of our adopted state and found ourselves at an outdoor art show. It was a glorious fall afternoon, and the park was packed with vendors showing their wares. For Vermont, the event had drawn a good crowd of people.

I remember feeling so happy and carefree, walking casually about. I looked out ahead, people-watching, and a familiar face jumped out from the others. A chill of what I thought was recognition ran through me, from scalp to fingertips and down to my toes. Some fifty feet before me was my first love, Frank—but it couldn't be. He lived in New Mexico now. I knew it could not be him, but it was.

He was walking right to me. I suddenly felt at ease and strangely calm. I reached out to my husband, who was but an arm's length away. At that moment I was stunned as my old flame walked, seemingly, right into me. I felt nothing but a wave of peace and contentment.

My husband had turned to see why I had paused, and I beseeched him, "Did you see that? That was Frank!" I turned to point out the "man" that had just passed, but he was gone. "He's disappeared!"

I felt a need to follow in the direction that "Frank" had gone. We ended up across the street from the park, in a used bookstore. It had been a huge house originally, and we wandered from room to room, browsing.

I felt that I was searching for something, but didn't know what it could be. In a dark hallway was a single bookcase, filled with dusty volumes that time had forgotten, one of which called to me. I picked it out and opened it to find a pressed four-leaf clover among the pages. A chill ran through me once again as I read the title page: *Natural Law in the Spirit World*. I bought the book.

A week later I received word that Frank had passed away the very day that I saw him in the park. I believe that he had come to say goodbye and make sure that I was happy in my life, assuring me good luck with the four-leaf clover and trying to give me understanding of life and death through the book.

Heather Froeschl
Roanoke, Virginia
September 2000

Sister, Goodbye

My sister Lavice was eighteen years old when I was born in Arbyrd, Missouri. There were no other children between us. Lavice and I had a relationship more like mother and daughter than like sisters and even her death hasn't been able to sever that bond.

As I grew up, married, and followed my sailor husband to various stations around the world our bond remained. If she was sick, I suffered her aches and pains. If she was happy, I felt happy. When she was depressed, I, too, would experience an emotional "down." Our frequent letters confirmed this empathy.

In 1962 my sister learned that she was dying of cancer. At that time she was living in Watsonville, California, and I was living in Washington, D.C. When the news reached me I immediately left for California. I drove to Missouri, packed my mother and younger brother into the car with my own two children, and we made what I thought was to be my last visit to my sister.

The disease finally took its toll and Lavice left her earthly body on February 16, 1963, shortly after her forty-first birthday. Her remains were returned to Missouri for burial.

The weather in Missouri had been balmy and warm until the day of Lavice's funeral. That day the temperature dropped to forty degrees. The flowers froze the instant they were placed around her grave, and I was beside myself with grief, agonizing inwardly because she was being placed in the hard, cold ground. It seemed so unfair that she had only those brief forty-one years on this earth.

The family members returned to our parents' home and we sat reminiscing quietly until late that night.

I had been asleep for maybe two hours when, suddenly, I found myself wide awake. I heard the front door quietly open and close. This seemed strange because no one else was up and the door had been dead-bolted from the inside. Then I once again felt that bone-chilling coldness I had felt at the cemetery.

My heart began to pound and I broke into a cold sweat. Softly but distinctly I could hear a steady footfall coming to my bedroom. As the footsteps approached nearer and nearer, I lay literally paralyzed with fear.

Then I saw her in the doorway. It was my sister! She was wearing the same dress she'd been buried in and she was looking at me and smiling. Slowly, she approached my bed and looked down at me. She leaned over and placed her hands on the covers at my shoulders. I could feel the icy cold of her touch. She kissed me softly on each cheek and said, "I just came to say goodbye. Don't be afraid. I'm not taking you with me. I will be so happy when you can come and be with me. Always remember that I love you."

Then she straightened up, turned around, and quietly walked out, leaving by the same door she had used when she entered.

The next morning I got up before the rest of the family and hurried to the front door. It was still dead-bolted from the inside. No one could possibly have entered the house that way the night before.

I didn't share this experience with anyone for several years. I even convinced myself that it was just a dream. When I finally told Dad about the strange occurrence, saying that I thought it must have been a dream, I saw that his eyes misted over.

"No, it was no dream. I heard the door and the footsteps, too, but I couldn't get out of bed. It was as if I was tied down. But I'm not at all surprised that she went to see you. She loved you more than anybody else in this world, and if she could say goodbye to any of us, it would have been to you."

Through the years I've never felt totally alone because I can still hear her soft voice telling me that she will be so happy when I can come and be with her.

Bonds Ridings
Burbank, California
May 1983

Gramps Kept His Promise

In the fall of 1943 I climbed into my old Ford to visit a friend who had recently lost her father-in-law. The funeral had taken place four months before but I had been too ill to attend.

As I drove along I began to realize how much Ruth and her six children would miss Gramps, for he had been their right-hand man. He always prepared the vegetables for dinner and helped with the dishes. He was such a cheerful person too. How he had enjoyed his prank of untying Ruth's apron at inopportune moments!

I recalled my last visit to the modest farm house on Route 1, out of Kokomo, Indiana. Gramps had hinted that his time was growing short but had vowed to return after death, if possible.

I turned into the narrow lane bordered with petunias and parked the car as usual at the side entrance. After kicking my way through colorful leaves, I rapped on the door. There was no answer. I rapped again and again. Suddenly, the door burst open. Ruth, white-faced and shaking, drew me inside.

"'Mary! Am I ever glad to see you! I've just had the most frightening experience."

Ruth told me she had just finished ironing in the living room and was carrying an armful of clothing to her bedroom. When she reached the doorway, she felt a slight tug on her apron strings. Her apron fell to the floor. After taking two or three steps into the bedroom, she turned about, puzzled. There, framed in the doorway, was Gramps with his familiar one-sided smile and his ever-present red bandana dangling from his jacket! The two surveyed each other for a moment.

"Is it really you, Gramps?" Ruth had whispered.

The figure nodded its head, smiled wistfully, and then it faded from view. Ruth, motionless with amazement, finally realized someone was knocking on the kitchen door. Gathering all her courage, she dashed to let me in.

As she finished telling me this, I looked past her into the living room. There, in the doorway to her bedroom, lay her crumpled apron!

Mary J. Arnett
Euclid, Ohio
December 1964

In Both Worlds

My proof of survival came through someone I scarcely knew. Eighteen years ago, Millie and Paul moved into the house next door. Pleasant, bothering no one, they soon became neighborhood favorites.

Shortly after they settled in, grief left them stunned. Their youngest child, eight-year-old, vibrant, pretty Nicole, died suddenly on a bright February morning.

In 1998, I saw Nicole, although I didn't recognize her at first. While reading in bed, I looked up and noticed a girl standing nearby. As I started, she smiled warmly and put fingers to her lips. She emanated such friendliness I instinctively realized she meant no harm. She reminded me of someone; I couldn't place whom. Slim and lithe, she had smartly coiffed red-gold hair and a glowing complexion.

I stared, fascinated and wondering, positive she came from another world, but not scared at all. In her mid-twenties, she had the poise and chic of a high-fashion model. Most impressive, however, was the deep contentment of her expression, smacking of religious dedication. Obviously she was on a mission and loving her role.

For perhaps half a minute, our eyes met. Then, moving swiftly, she wrote a couple of sentences on a white sheet of paper and deposited it at my side, not touching me. There was a sense of an impassable gap between us. Drawing back, she vanished. No fading—one instant she was present, the next, not. Ditto the paper.

When I told Millie of her visit she asked, "How was she dressed?"

"In a sky-blue frock. A classy job. It had fancy buttons. Silk, I think."

"She was buried in one like that. And this is the anniversary of her death!"

"But why didn't she leave a message?" I asked.

"Oh, she did, Wyn. She radiated God's peace and happiness. Plainly she's with Him and also with us. What could be better than that!"

Wyn Esselborn
Newark, New Jersey
April 2000

Warnings
Saved by the Dead

There is a particular episode of the animated TV comedy *The Simpsons* involving the family's trip to the funeral of a distant relative, in which Homer Simpson finds it necessary to sternly remind his son Bart not to disrespect the dead. He backs up his fatherly rebuke with information obviously obtained from Grade Z horror movies: "Don't mess with the dead, boy. They have eerie powers," he asserts with goofy sincerity.

This is played for laughs, of course. But the readers who contributed the following reports would probably agree with the substance of Homer's statement. Those "eerie powers"—specifically, the ability to foresee dangerous or difficult situations—are used for the benefit of living loved ones in these stories.

Hunter's Angel

After Mom's untimely passing in 1957, Dad had her portrait framed in gold and placed it on the mantle as a constant reminder of the way she always watched over her family.

In December 1964, I was in Pennsylvania's Pocono Mountains hunting deer with my wife's uncle and cousins as guests of the local rod and gun club. While the others visited with friends at the clubhouse, I hunted alone. Because I was unfamiliar with the area, I stuck to an old dirt trail. Suddenly I saw Mom, thirty yards to my right, among the tree shadows, but only her head and shoulders were visible, as though her portrait had been transported to this spot without the gold frame, and suspended a foot above the ground.

I stood dumbstruck, not knowing what was happening, or why. Then I remembered my binoculars and lifted them to my eyes—there she was, smiling at me.

"Hello Mom," I said silently, expecting some kind of message, but none came. I watched and waited for what seemed like five minutes, but what I later realized was probably not more than thirty seconds. Then, slowly, her image faded. "Goodbye, Mom," I said. "Thank you for the visit."

Still puzzled, I tried to go on hunting. I resumed my slow pace, but before I covered fifty yards, a rifle shot rang out from the top of the hillside on my left.

I heard the bullet smack into a tree at head height twenty yards ahead of me, and saw bark chips fly. Then, I knew why Mom was there. She only had to delay me long enough to avoid a meeting with that bullet, and she did it in a way that I was able to accept. There was no doubt in my mind that I would not have walked away from that place without her intervention. I made no effort to identify the shooter. I exited as quickly and quietly as possible, telling no one at the clubhouse.

That memory stirs up many emotions. Mom's visit remains very comforting, even after all these years. I know she still watches over her family.

John Blasi
Apache Junction, Arizona
June 1994

"Tell Dave Forty-Seven"

At the beginning of 1991, I embarked on a new career—the high-stakes game called commodity futures trading. Simply put, this involves buying contracts on commodities (like corn, soybeans, gold, or oil) for future delivery at, hopefully, a higher price. I specialized in grains, where one contract was five thousand bushels. I had positions in several grains, but my largest was corn, in which I had five hundred thousand bushels. A price change of one cent resulted in a profit or loss of five thousand dollars. After five years I had turned five thousand dollars into three hundred thousand dollars.

That's the background; now here's the story. It was the weekend and I was spending it at home with Shirley, my extremely psychic girlfriend. Both my parents have passed over, but occasionally they "drop in" and give Shirley a message to pass on to me. One of these messages came on a night that I had gone to bed early and left Shirley to spend the night watching television. The following morning, she told me she had been talking to my dad. He had said, "Tell Dave forty-seven," and pointed to the wall. There was a red "47" on the wall.

I tried to figure it out. I reasoned that since I was dealing in large amounts of money, and since the "47" was red, it had to mean a loss. I was going to hit a wall and lose money. But what about the "47"? Could it be the fourth day of the seventh month? No—that was Independence Day, and the markets were closed. Could it be the seventh day of the fourth month, or maybe forty-seven days?

I counted the days off on the calendar. The forty-seventh day was April 16—my dad's birthday. *Too much of a coincidence*, I thought, and ruled it out. It had to be April 7—the seventh day of the fourth month. But that day came and went, and nothing unusual happened.

On April 16, the forty-seventh day, the price of corn dropped like the proverbial rock. There were no buyers, and the price of corn fell twelve cents, as did the other grains. The next day the price dropped another eight cents before I could get out. I was wiped out. Everything I had made over the past five years was gone. Now, too late, I understood the message from my dad.

This is just one of the many episodes that prove for me that life does not end with death.

David E. Irving
Hamilton, Ontario, Canada
November 2000

Lady of the Third Dimension

World War II was in its second year in 1942, and our men were away fighting for their country. I was fifteen years old and living in a small three-room apartment in the heart of staid old Boston with Mother, who is a solid, no-nonsense person with green eyes, freckles, and naturally curly red hair that I have always envied. This particular weekend my paternal grandmother was visiting us. Grandmother fascinated me. A showgirl in her youth, she was still very beautiful with snow-white hair, black eyes, and a flawless olive complexion. From my earliest recollection there had been a strong bond between us, and I was happy to relinquish my bed to her and sleep on the couch in the front room.

I remember going to bed early as we proposed to go shopping the next morning. Sometime during the night I was awakened by someone gently stroking my forehead. Sitting on the edge of my couch was a petite, exotic-looking woman with beautiful, piercing black eyes. Her hair, shimmering in the moonlight from the open window, was blue-black and hung loosely to her waist. She wore what appeared to be an old-fashioned flannel nightgown trimmed with lace and blue ribbons. Her slender finger lay across her lips signalling me to be quiet.

She seemed to sense my fright and smiled warmly; she made no move toward me nor did she speak. She just hovered protectively over me. Nevertheless my terror mounted. I lay in a cold sweat, my eyes following her every move. It seemed an eternity before she slowly rose, still smiling, and floated into oblivion. I wanted to cry out but my mouth was parched, my throat paralyzed. The next thing I remember was Mother saying, "C'mon, sister, it's time to get up."

Mother and Grandmother were already sipping their second cup of coffee as I sat down.

"Sister, you are awfully pale this morning. Didn't you sleep well?" Grandmother asked.

"I had a bad nightmare," I replied. And then I related the details as carefully as I could.

Grandmother paled noticeably and said, "No, child, this was not a dream but a visitation. You will see her again! Hear me out, for I have seen her on a number of occasions.

"My most vivid recollection concerns my brother George, a broad-shouldered, freckled-faced, redheaded giant of a man. At twenty, George left home and went to Chicago to make his way. There he obtained employment and lived in a boardinghouse. George never had been sick a day in his life, yet one morning he did not show up for work.

"His landlady was busy with her daily chores when the doorbell rang. When she answered she was surprised to see a young priest in a long black cassock who asked if he could see the young man who was dying.

"'But, Father, I only have one male roomer and he went to work this morning,' she said.

"The priest begged her to check, saying that a lovely young woman had appeared at the registry that morning and informed them that a young man was dying and in dire need of assistance. She had given them this address. Together the priest and the landlady climbed the stairs to George's second-floor room. The door was ajar, and they entered. George's clothes were folded neatly on the chair and his wallet lay open on the oval-top table. George was in bed, lying flat on his back, unable to move.

"In a barely audible voice George inquired, 'Father, how did you know I was sick? Who sent you?'

"The priest told him the same story he had told the landlady. Then, realizing the seriousness of George's condition, he administered the last rites. Afterwards his gaze fell on a large oil painting of Mother that hung over George's bed.

"'That is the woman who came to the rectory this morning. Where is she?' he asked.

"George looked puzzled. 'That is my mother, sir. She died when I was a baby.'

"'Impossible!' said the priest, 'I shook hands with her. She was warm and very much alive.'

"Two hours later George was dead. We brought him home and buried him in a grave next to Mother.

"Now, my child," Grandmother continued, "I want you to promise me you will be most careful in everything you do for the next few weeks."

On a lazy spring morning about two weeks later I headed for the bus stop with some of my young friends. We were running, shoving and pushing one another. At the bus stop, standing with her back toward us, was a petite woman in a pink dress, her black hair neatly pulled back in a French twist. There was something familiar about her, but I paid little attention. We could see the bus coming. As it drew close someone shoved me and to my horror I felt myself falling in front of the oncoming machine. Then someone grabbed me, shortening my fall. Badly shaken, I turned to thank my rescuer, and found myself gazing into the face that had hovered over my couch a few nights before. It was such a shock that I passed out and in the ensuing confusion the woman disappeared. No one had bothered to get her name but I knew who she was. God help me, I knew!

Several times since then I have been visited by my great-grandmother, Agnes Elizabeth Riley Murray, born in County Cork, Ireland. Each time she has warned me of impending danger. On several occasions these warnings have saved my life.

Then a few years ago the postman brought me a letter from my own son, who was then in Vietnam. The letter told of his being separated from his buddies in the jungle and of a sudden encounter with a beautiful woman with flashing black eyes and long black hair. He wrote that she saved his life by delaying his progress through the tropical forest. Then she disappeared.

"I know, Mother, you will think me insane," he wrote.

But of course, I know he wrote the truth. He, too, has experienced our family's protector—my beautiful great-grandmother.

Agnes Smith
El Paso, Texas
March 1974

"Mom, Please"

My daughter, Mildred Crow, died on June 11, 1963, at 1:50 A.M. I did not have the money to attend her funeral in Texas and remained at my home in Vienna, Ohio.

At 10:00 P.M. on July 19, a little more than a month after Mildred died, I was settling down to sleep when I felt someone sit down on my bed. I turned to see if it was my sick husband wanting something and I saw Mildred sitting there, on the edge of my bed!

She said, "Mom, go to the doctor."

I told her, "Honey, I am all right. I don't need a doctor."

Mildred left but she came again the next night. She insisted that I see the doctor. Again, I told her that I didn't need the doctor.

The third night she reappeared saying, "Mom, please. See Doctor Bill before it is too late!"

I promised my daughter that I would see our family doctor, whose name is Bill, in the morning. He sent me right to the hospital for emergency treatment for diabetes. He said that if I had delayed seeing him one more week it would have been too late to do anything but make me comfortable until the end.

I love my daughter and find she is closer to me now than she was before.

Florence Ague
Tice, Florida
September 1965

King Oswald's Gray

On Christmas Eve, 1959, I drove along the old Roman road between Greenhead and Newcastle-upon-Tyne. The night was wet but I was anxious to reach home and help the children decorate the Christmas tree, and so I pushed my car at a fast clip.

Suddenly my mother put her hand on my shoulder and said, "Steady, Son, there is danger ahead."

Puzzled and excited at seeing her again—for Sarah Ann Schofield, my mother, had been dead for some years—I turned to speak to her. She had disappeared.

I shrugged off the incident as being a hallucination brought on by fatigue and continued on. I was still musing over the incident when my headlights illuminated a group of horses trotting across the road. I hit the brakes but because of my speed I was sure I couldn't avoid them. My auto slid toward them and right on through the last of the horses.

When the car came to a stop I climbed out and walked to the side of the road to see where the horses had gone. To my astonishment, there was no sign of them and no marks or breaks in the hedge that lined both sides of the road.

Getting back into the car, I glanced up the road to see a huge log stretched across it. It was a large piece of tree trunk, newly felled, about four feet long. With considerable difficulty I rolled it into the hedge. I surmise it had fallen off a logger's lorry.

Had I continued into the log at the speed I was traveling, I never would have been home for Christmas.

After the holidays I told a friend, Professor D. Russel, a lecturer in psychology at Newcastle University, about my Christmas Eve experiences.

When I described the place where I had seen the horses, he told me that King Oswald of Northumbria had fought a battle at that spot in A.D. 600. There is a cross by the road-side commemorating this event, but I had not known about it.

Our conversation cleared up a small mystery in connection with the horses. One horse, a gray, had had a leather piece over its back. This was not like a modern saddle but was just a simple leather piece with loops for stirrups. The design and markings on it had been quite clear and distinct, with the colors blue, red, and green. Professor Russel explained that the design and colored markings as I described them were of a saddle worn more than one thousand years ago when King Oswald was riding into battle.

James Schofield (as told to Mary Crowe)
Bristol, England
January 1967

Phone Call from Beyond

For many years my friend Davis Stone was sole caretaker of a large mansion and estate next door to me on Belmont Street in Indianapolis, Indiana. His daughter Ruby and I had been great pals before she died when she was only seven. In 1969 Davis fell from a ladder and as a result was nearly crippled. If he sat bent over or in an unusual position for any length of time he would be unable to work for days or even weeks.

Not long after his fall Davis's employers went on vacation and Davis had complete responsibility for the estate. The job was really too much for one person, and I was continually on the watch to see that he did not cripple himself again. One evening just before dusk my telephone rang and I answered it. I heard a voice I recognized but could not place; it was the tiny voice of a child.

She said, "They told me I could not telephone but I just did, didn't I?"

Puzzled, I said, "I know your voice but who are you?"

"You know me," she answered. "I am Ruby!"

"Thank you and goodbye," I said as I dropped the phone, alarmed that something must be wrong with Davis. I heard the little voice say, "Thank you too."

I dashed next door and tried to get in. There was no answer to my knock but I found a door that was unlatched and went from room to room to see what was the matter.

On a big chair I found Davis, sound asleep in a position that would have crippled him. Suddenly I knew he could not be awakened quickly so I just stood nearby and repeated his name. Finally he awoke and said, "Oh, my back! It's a good thing you came to see about me, but what is the reason?"

Stunned for a moment at the immensity of the answer I must give, I finally said, "Your daughter Ruby called me on the telephone."

Disbelief showed on his face. I couldn't blame him. The truth staggered me too when I realized what it meant.

"My phone is still off the hook," I added. "I dropped it when I knew something was wrong over here. Ruby said 'Thank you' just as I dashed over. She was still on the line."

Davis and I agreed this was very like Ruby. She always had been so careful to observe the pleasantries of life.

I am careful to whom I tell this story, but the telephone call from beyond remains a rare treasure in my memory.

Viola Tollen
Indianapolis, Indiana
July 1974

Obeying His Command

My mother lived with me in the 1940s in the village of Pacheco, California. She often went to San Jose by bus to visit another daughter, and on these occasions we planned that I would pick her up at the Greyhound bus station in Concord, two miles away, when she returned. Her only delay was a two-hour wait in Oakland to change buses. She made the trip often, always returning well and happy.

One Saturday that Mother was due in Concord at four o'clock in the afternoon was a busy day for me, a school-teacher, and about one o'clock I was ironing when I heard my father's voice: "Mabel, go get your mother."

How could that be? I thought. I knew my father's voice instantly—although he had been dead for more than five years. "Stop dreaming and get on with your chores," I told myself.

My father's voice came again, this time with great emphasis and unmistakable urgency: "Mabel, go get your mother!"

Something was wrong somewhere—no doubt of that. I could not disobey his insistent command. I disconnected the iron and ran into the living room where a young visiting nephew was painting.

"Lane," I said, "we have to go to Oakland and we have to hurry."

It was only early afternoon. I knew right away I must go to Oakland. Mother's bus wouldn't reach Concord until four.

When we arrived at the bus station, the San Jose to Oakland bus was just pulling in. Mother, the first passenger off, wore a happy smile and looked around the station as if expecting someone to meet her. When she saw me through the glass door, her smile faded.

As we embraced she said in a disappointed tone, "A nice man was going to meet me—but he said if anyone else met me, he wouldn't show up."

I had a hunch that my father's urgent command had forestalled real tragedy. Ushering Mother into the waiting room, I said, "Tell me all about this."

"Well, I met him a few days ago. He said we would be married right away, then leave at once for Florida where he had a beautiful estate."

I interrupted: "Mother, did you tell him you owned some property?"

"Yes," she admitted in some confusion.

"We will wait a few minutes longer, then go home." I said.

Her instant lover did not appear so we picked up Lane at the newsstand and went home. We never referred to this incident again, but I often saw Mother looking out a window as if she expected someone to come.

Three months later, the newspapers carried an account of a man who enticed elderly women into marriage with promises of a beautiful estate in Florida. He had been jailed for murder, for poisoning those would-be wives on the way south. The man's picture appeared in the paper and I showed it to Mother, asking, "Mother, is this the man?"

Shocked into tears, she answered, "Yes."

Irene Mabel McDonald
Paradise, California
October 1984

The Man in Black

When I was a teenager we lived in Kalamazoo, Michigan, in the last house on a court. The houses all were large and old, and no doubt many children have run and played in that court.

One summer afternoon in 1935 or '36 a storm was brewing. The sky was growing dark and the huge oak trees that lined our court made it even darker there. My two sisters, Ruth and Phyllis, and several neighbor girls were playing a made-up game that consisted mostly of chasing each other back and forth to the end of the court, screaming a lot. I was a little old for such kid games but that day I had "lowered my dignity" to join in the fun.

As lightning crackled directly overhead and thunder sounded almost instantly behind it, we decided we had time to make only one more dash to the end of the court before the rain came. We had run only a short way when we all came to a sudden halt. Directly in front of us under the biggest oak tree was a man dressed all in black. His wide-brimmed hat and ankle-length coat were from a long-ago past. The wide brim of the hat shaded his face so we could not see his features. Seconds before, he had not been there and we couldn't understand where he had come from. Yet there he was, arm and palm held outward as if to warn us to go back. And go back we did, racing and stumbling onto our front porch.

We just had reached the front steps when a bolt of lightning blazed downward and with an earsplitting crash struck the pavement where we would have been at that moment if the man in black had not frightened us into racing home. The concussion felt like a hand slammed into my back. Screaming, we turned to see where the man in black was. But there was no man! Only the smell of sulphur hung in the air and the rain came down in torrents.

Our father, hearing the noise, came running out and when we told him our story he dashed to the end of the court to see if he could see the man in black. But there was no one anywhere on the street.

Where the tall stranger came from and where he went we'll never know, but we'll remember him. If it hadn't been for him we would not be here today.

Barbara Carrothers
Coloma, Michigan
August 1976

Brother-in-Law's Warning

February 1992 was a devastating time for my family. My son-in-law Robert died in a scuba-diving accident at age thirty. My daughter Meryl was left to raise their son Daniel, who was only five months old at the time. It has taken years for her to recover from her grief.

One evening in May of that year, I was knitting and watching one of my favorite TV programs. Out of the corner of my eye I saw a slight movement. Glancing across the room, I saw Robert standing in the doorway, a huge grin on his face. I sat motionless, longing to turn off the TV, but frightened in case any move would cause me to lose him.

I smiled at him and we had a conversation that took place in our heads. I didn't speak at all, but the communication was as clear as if we were talking. I told him how we all missed him, especially Meryl, and I asked him to please help her to cope with her life now. As he had been an experienced diver, and the Royal Canadian Mounted Police had found nothing wrong with his diving gear, I asked him what had happened. He said it had been his own fault, as he had been careless.

He then told me he had come to give me a message for my son Rob, who lives in Thailand. I was surprised, as the two young men had only met a few times. Robert stated quite clearly, "Tell Rob that if he doesn't change his life soon, he could end up with me in the near future."

I wanted to ask Robert more questions, but he had gone. I turned off the TV and sat for a long time marveling at what had happened.

I didn't dare tell the family about Robert's visit, as it seemed so unbelievable. (It was several years before I even broached the subject with Meryl, but when I did she was not surprised. She feels his presence too, occasionally, and sees tiny flashes of blue light when he is near.) After a week of wrestling with my thoughts, I decided to phone my son—and risk him thinking his mother had completely lost her mind. I knew Rob had recently started a new job that he really enjoyed. His life had sounded fine when I had last spoken to him.

Rob was surprised to hear from me, as we had spoken only a few weeks before. I told him he must promise not to think me insane, and then I related the facts of his brother-in-law's visit.

There was silence on the other end of the phone, long enough for me to ask if he was still there. When Rob finally spoke, he sounded shaken. He told me he had kept the details of his life from me, as he didn't want me to worry.

Rob wanted to end a relationship with a girl he had dated for almost a year. He had tried several times in recent months to talk to her, but she told him she would commit suicide if he ever left her. She was extremely possessive and questioned his every move. The situation had now worsened—her father had threatened Rob with death if he deserted his daughter. My son felt his life was spinning out of control.

I urged Rob to return to Canada immediately, but he said he would never forgive himself if his girlfriend carried out her suicide threat. I told him she was just using that as a hold on him and it was most unlikely she would go through with it once he had left. (I was later proved to be right, as she apparently found another boyfriend soon after Rob left.)

Rob was back in Canada within days. He left Thailand at night and did not even dare to tell his employer where he was going in case word got back to the irate father. Rob stayed with me for a month, and then returned to Thailand, settling hundreds of miles from where he had lived previously.

As the years go by the memory of Robert's visit stays vividly in my memory. Today my son is happily married and is the father of an eighteen-month-old daughter. I know we have Robert to thank for his happiness.

Margaret Davies
Medicine Hat, Alberta, Canada
August 2001

Unfinished Business
Promises Kept; Tasks Completed after Death

Death is the ultimate interruption—the deadline of all deadlines. What is left undone at the time of passing is, to the "rational," commonsense view, beyond completion.

Or is it?

The following stories indicate that sometimes, responsibility for one's loved ones and promises is strong enough to survive the transition. Departed spirits may return to mark significant anniversaries, to resolve conflicts before moving on, or to provide assistance to a person in need. Whatever the nature of the afterlife, these stories speak to an emotional connection between this life and the next.

Jimmy, Is That You?

In the summer of 1966, when I was seventeen, my nineteen-year-old cousin James Kajiwara and I spent endless hours discussing our plans for the future. Then Jimmy was drafted into the army. His eventual destination was Vietnam. Before leaving for advanced infantry training at Fort Benning, Georgia, he gave me my Christmas, birthday, and graduation presents.

"Roy," he said, "I have a feeling I won't be back."

"Don't say that!" I pleaded. "Promise me you'll be back for my graduation next June."

"Okay, I promise. I'll be back."

But four months later, on March 11, 1967, he was killed in action. I tried to deny his death. At first I felt empty, then angry; finally I felt nothing. Graduation day came and thoughts of Jimmy welled up inside me. The graduating students sat up in the hot bleachers of the Tennyson High School gym while the parents were seated on the main floor. Wiping the sweat off my face, I watched the setting sun cast an eerie light through the doors.

Suddenly a chill swept through my whole body as if someone had dumped a bucket of ice water on my head. I began to shiver uncontrollably. I looked for Mom down in the audience—and then I saw him. Standing in the doorway, just two hundred feet away, was Jimmy. A wave of heat engulfed my body. Quickly I looked away in fear.

The student sitting next to me said, "What's the matter? Looks like you just saw a ghost."

Though panic-stricken, I summoned my courage and looked at Jimmy again. He was wearing his favorite red Pendleton shirt, carrying his camera as usual, and smiling directly at me.

"Do you see that guy standing over there at the door?" I asked my neighbor.

"What guy? Are you all right?" he replied.

But it wasn't a dream. All I could manage was to smile at Jimmy, and then he was gone. My heart sank. Who would ever believe me?

Several days later, when I couldn't hold it inside any longer, I confided in Mom (Lillian Matsuda).

"Tell me when and where you saw him," she said. "What did he look like?"

Slowly I repeated the details of my experience to her.

"I thought it was a dream but I know it wasn't."

"It was no dream," Mom said, "because you're describing exactly what I saw too."

I was relieved and stunned all at once. Heretofore I had never had any feelings about life after death. Jimmy came back to show me the truth.

Roy Matsuda (as told to Corliss Chan)
Larkspur, California
February 1986

Visiting Grandparents

My ex-husband was a violent bully during our marriage, and after one particularly heavy beating, I crawled back to bed and just lay there. I knew that if my three-year-old son wakened from his afternoon sleep, I would not be able to go to him.

I was past crying and just asked Spirit, and my departed father, for help. Suddenly, very gently, someone sat on the bed, stroked my head, and held me in unseen arms. I fell asleep and awakened about five hours later, feeling a lot better.

I heard my son laughing, and went to him. As I entered the sitting room, he was waving goodbye to someone. Looking around I saw that not only had he been entertained, but he had also been given snacks. He had obviously had a great afternoon. Somehow I knew I did not have to worry.

I asked him who had been there, and he pointed to a photo of my parents—Gran and Granpa had spent the afternoon with him, he said.

They were always there for me when they were alive, and I know they are still there for us.

Pat Kennedy
Glasgow, Scotland
September 2000

Plea for Forgiveness

We were living on a farm near Tulsa, Oklahoma, in July 1921. The noise of the men and machinery in the process of baling bluestem hay came with the breeze through the open kitchen window, where, shortly before ten o'clock, I was busy cooking the noon meal for a crew of hungry men. My three children were in an adjoining room.

As I worked, I thought about my mother in Indiana, who slowly was dying of cancer of the liver. Until my husband David and I had moved west, we all had lived in the same house. Not a doting grandmother, my mother had made my life pretty miserable after the birth of each child.

A hush fell over the place. I glanced through the window and saw the men standing around the water keg, I stepped to the door of the next room to see what my children were doing. I gasped. There on my low rocker sat my mother, with her arms around my children.

Memory of her pain-ravaged face as it turned toward me still brings tears to my eyes. Her eyes were pleading silently for forgiveness and love.

The vision was like a flash—gone in an instant, but as real as life.

When my astonished eyes could focus again, I saw my oldest child lying on the floor reading, his feet propped in a chair. His sisters sat on the floor, dressing their dolls. They were unaware of the shock I had received.

I forgot to bake pie that day and was scolded for my negligence. I never did tell my husband of this experience; he would have laughed. But that pleading look in my mother's eyes meant more to me than pies.

That same evening a telegram came. It said: "Your mother died this morning at ten minutes of ten o'clock."

Ellen Blazier
Claremore, Oklahoma
December 1964

The Missing Documents

My grandmother Lotte Langden had a suit pending in 1920 over some of her real-estate holdings in Wisconsin. Her lawyer Herbert Marshall asked her several times for a certain document fixing the debatable borders of the estate in litigation but Grandmother stubbornly refused to turn over the paper supporting her claims. "I'll hold on to this paper if I die over it," she stated. "There is no use risking it out of my hands."

That July she did die, suddenly one evening at supper while the whole family was present. Now Mr. Marshall had not only the pending suit but also the settlement of her estate on his busy hands. We searched all over the house for her legal papers but without success. The lack of the critical document deprived Mr. Marshall of his most potent argument in court, but along with the rest of her documents it was missing and we feared Grandmother had taken the secret of its hiding place with her to the grave.

On the fourth day after her death Mr. Marshall had joined the family for dinner and was lamenting the old lady's stubbornness and his futile fight in court. Dinner was being served by our maid Berthe, who had been with the family for forty years. In the midst of the meal our conversation was interrupted by a loud scream from Berthe followed by the sound of shattering dishes in the hallway.

We rushed to the hallway through which Berthe passed on her way from the kitchen and found her standing among the ruins of a sumptuous supper, white and trembling, pointing toward the highbacked chair that stood next to the old-fashioned grandfather clock. Grandmother had so often rested in this chair after she came in from a walk or from puttering in her garden that the family jokingly referred to it as her "throne."

When Berthe finally was calm enough to talk coherently she claimed that as she passed through the hallway with the tray of food she had seen Grandmother sitting on her "throne," gently stroking the grandfather clock. We talked excitedly about this but Mr. Marshall called Berthe an hysterical old fool and turned the conversation to more mundane matters.

Perhaps we might have forgotten the incident if we had not been forcefully reminded of it the very next evening when the same thing recurred. When Berthe was walking through the hallway she again saw Grandmother seated on the chair and again she dropped her tray.

The matter grew frightening when the same thing was repeated on the third night. The excitement only added to our concern over the pending trial that would begin in only two days now. Mr. Marshall was running in circles trying to find either the missing document or some other proof that would clinch the case.

After the third appearance of Grandmother's apparition, however, Grandfather William Langden, a cool practical man who at first attributed Berthe's visions to her long, close relationship to the family, said to us: "Listen, my dears. I wonder—perhaps it's ridiculous but no harm can come from it—if Grandmama did not want to tell us where her missing papers are. She stroked the clock—let's search within."

We did, and behold! In a hidden double back behind the swinging pendulum were Grandmother's papers! The suit was won and Berthe received an ample reward in addition to her set-out share in Grandmother's will. And never again was Grandmother seen to occupy her "throne."

Paul C. Langden (as told to Hereward Carrington)
Chicago, Illinois
April 1974

What Had He Left Behind?

When I was a child, my grandfather John Collson lived with us in our home in Erin, New York. He was bedridden and finally died in the spring of 1949. During his lengthy illness he used to holler "Hello!" whenever he wanted anything. As his condition became worse, the frequency of his calls increased and whoever was nearby would try to tend to his needs.

After he died we continued to hear his voice and his familiar call of "Hello!" Everyone in the house heard it. We searched the house many times to find any unusual sound that might be misinterpreted as his voice—but we found nothing. My mother insisted that it was a trick of memory but we children were convinced it was Grandfather's ghost.

The climax came Christmas Eve 1949, when the adults all were out of the house. My cousin, my brother and sister, our dog, and I were home alone. Our German shepherd was a bit too friendly to excel as a watchdog but nevertheless she always raised an alarm if strangers were near the house at night.

We all heard the first noise from Grandfather's room. The dog bristled, then whined as she took refuge behind the davenport. Her unusual behavior scared us more than the original noise. It sounded as if someone were searching frantically through the room. Drawers banged and the closet door slammed—then silence. The dog crawled from her hiding place and four terrified youngsters began to relax and search for an explanation. We checked the room and found nothing out of place. The only window was closed and locked from the inside.

That was the last manifestation of any kind from Grandfather's room. Never again did we hear his voice.

We don't know what caused the disturbance but the four of us like to believe that Grandfather found what he was looking for and now has no more reason to return.

J. M. Swan
Pine Valley, New York
September 1967

Final Flight

At three o'clock the morning after we buried my dad, Thomas Hogan, in Queens, New York, the front door slammed and the large mirror over the sideboard in the dining room hit the floor. It did not break or shatter.

For fifteen years, Dad had slammed that door at three o'clock after a night out in his favorite tavern. My mother Ruth Hogan often scolded him, saying that one day the mirror would fall. But it never had—until now.

My grandfather William O'Shea and I were frightened but nevertheless we started down the stairs. We stopped when we heard the door to the basement close and foot-steps going down the stairs. Continuing on down, we saw the mirror. We went to the basement door but could hear nothing. We locked the door and decided to wait until day-light for further action.

After Mother's suicide by hanging the year before, on January 4, 1948, Dad had chosen to sleep in the basement. He also hanged himself there—on June 18, 1949, when he was forty-six years old.

The next morning Grandfather and I continued our search and thought the strange, pungent smell of death was present. We checked the two windows in the basement bed-room; they were locked and so was the one in the laundry area. We looked at each other and decided to forget it.

That same afternoon I was out in the backyard with my son Kenneth when I heard something hitting those same bedroom windows. I was amazed to see a fairly large bird frantically trying to break through the glass from the inside. I called out to Grandpa, asking him to go down to the basement and unlock the back door.

A few seconds later, after Grandpa had joined us in the garden, the bird flew out. It circled over our heads three times, then perched on the garden gate nearby, watching us. When I said, "You are free to go," the bird circled my head once more, then flew away.

Life with Dad had not been easy. I had the strange feeling he was asking for forgiveness now that his spirit was going to another plane.

Eleanore Page
St. Petersburg, Florida
January 1988

On the Midnight Shift

I experienced quite a few unexplainable events on the midnight shift during my thirteen years as a New York City police officer.

One night about eight years ago, Central sent my partner and me on a call for an apparent break-in. The house where the alarm had sounded was an old, three-story A-frame. It had a window up in the third-floor attic that faced the street. My partner and I exited the patrol car and searched the outside of the property for evidence of a break-in. We didn't notice anything unusual in the yard or outside of the house, so we proceeded to the front door.

I knocked on the door, and stepped away to check the windows. In the third-floor attic window I saw the blinds get pushed to the side, and I could barely make out the face of someone looking down at us.

I said to my partner, "It's going to be a minute; they're up on the third floor."

Before I finished saying that, the front door began to open. An old woman asked us to come in. We proceeded into the home. She had three dogs that barked incessantly. After a brief conversation, she stated she was living alone.

Since I had seen someone up on the third floor, it meant that she really was not alone. We didn't want to alarm the woman, so we told her we wanted to check out the house, just to be sure.

After checking the first floor, we told her we wanted to check upstairs. As we walked toward the stairs to the second floor I asked her, "Have you ever had a problem with the alarm before?" She told me that the only other time it kept going off for no apparent reason was on the night of her husband's birthday.

We continued up the stairs, not thinking anything of her response. She then said that it was odd, because tonight was the one-year anniversary of his death! My partner and I shot each other a look and thought something strange was going on.

We searched the second floor and didn't find anything. The windows were locked tight, just like on the first floor, and there was no apparent sign of a break-in to trigger the alarm.

There was just one other floor to check. From what I had seen earlier, I knew there was someone upstairs.

I asked her how to get into the attic. She pointed at a door and said, "Behind that door there's a flight of stairs."

I looked at my partner; he said he was not going up there!

I wasn't too happy, but since I definitely saw someone I wasn't going to leave.

I proceeded up the stairs, found the switch, and turned on the light. It was apparent no one had been up there for a long time. It was a big, dark, empty attic.

I went to the window that faced the street. It was locked, as was the window that faced the back.

After searching the attic, I told her the alarm must have malfunctioned because no one was in her home. We told her to call us if it ever happened again. We didn't want to tell her what it really was: her late husband paying her a visit!

Ed Thorgersen
Holtsville, New York
June 2001

Strings from Heaven

At the age of nineteen, Kenneth Null, the boy next door in Bells, Tennessee, showed great promise as a concert violinist. Then tragedy struck. Ken was involved in an automobile accident that cost him the use of his right arm. Everything possible was done for him. Doctor after doctor was consulted, but always it was the same story: he never would play again. Friends and relatives tried to interest him in another career, but he wouldn't listen. He insisted he would play again.

"I will play again," he told me one night when we were alone. "If I didn't believe that, I wouldn't want to live."

Suddenly I, too, believed. I told myself I was being foolish, but it didn't keep me from sharing his hope.

A few weeks later, on June 5, 1948, I heard the violin at midnight. Ken was playing again. The music was heavenly.

"Wake up," I called to my sister, Lydia. "Ken is playing his violin, and he's at home alone. He will need someone to share his triumph."

We raced across the lawn, putting on our housecoats as we ran. The front door was unlocked, so we stepped inside and stood listening. Ken was playing in the den. Never had we heard more beautiful music.

Then the music stopped. We burst through the door with tears and shouts of joy, but Ken didn't answer. He lay motionless on the couch with his beloved violin pressed against his heart.

The doctor later told us that when we found him he had been dead at least two hours from a cerebral hemorrhage. My sister and I didn't argue. Dead or alive, Ken had played again, for himself and for the two people who still had shared his hope and faith.

M. L. Lovett
Gastonia, North Carolina
December 1964

Still in the Family

In the late 1970s I belonged to an enthusiastic southern California group known as PSI, or Psychic Science Investigators. There were between fifteen and twenty of us. One of our activities was to visit old houses in the area and tune in on them psychically. I was in charge of these investigative tours.

Among the historical sites we visited was Newland House in Huntington Beach. We went through it, room by room, to see what "vibrations" we could pick up and to keep mentally alert for any possible psychic phenomena.

When our group went through the Newland home, I was careful to explain to the docents—volunteers who take visitors on tours of the historic residence—that we would like to walk through the building without being given any information about the rooms or anything in them. We also asked and received permission to use the psychic gift of psychometry, which meant we could touch or handle objects to gain psychic impressions from them. We did all this and jotted down our impressions.

After our exploration we decided to meditate around the large dining room table. Sometimes, in the altered state induced by meditation, it becomes easier to pick up thought forms or spirits who may be present. We had a video camera with us and used it to record the proceedings.

At one point during our meditation the chandelier over the table began to swing back and forth. We all saw this and so did the docents who were seated outside our circle. Yet when we played back the videotape the chandelier was not shown moving.

As we continued to meditate I could sense a spirit standing by my right shoulder. I could see her clairvoyantly very clearly. The figure was that of an old woman wearing a long lavender dress. She had white hair done in a bun and she was leaning on a cane. In my mind I could hear her voice. In a querulous tone she said she wanted me to ask a question for her.

"My portrait is missing from this home," she said and added, "It was in a large oval, dark-colored frame. I want it put back."

So I interrupted the meditation and described the woman to the group. Then I described the portrait and asked if anyone there knew what had happened to it.

Since no one seemed to know anything about the matter, the meditation resumed. When it was over the spirit appeared again at my right side. And again she insisted I ask about her portrait.

"The old lady is back again," I said to everybody in the room, "and I don't think she will go away until she gets an answer. Can anyone help?"

At this one of the docents, Bess Kennedy, who had accompanied us through the house, turned red and stammered, "I have it."

Everyone looked at her in surprise.

"I have it," she repeated. And then she confessed: "Before I was married my maiden name was Newland. The old lady you described to us was my grandmother. When Newland

House was given to the county as an historical site, I wanted to have my grandmother's portrait, so I took it home with me. Yes, it looked exactly as it was described, but now it is in a square frame instead of the oval walnut frame it had originally."

She looked at the other docents and said firmly, "I'm not giving it back!"

I told her she would have to work that out with her departed grandmother.

At this point the spirit disappeared. Maybe she was satisfied knowing her portrait was still in the family

Christine Metzner
Fullerton, California
January 1986

Checking Out the Bride

On Friday, December 11, 1998, I went to bed early, hoping to get a good night's sleep. At about 2:00 A.M., I woke up for no apparent reason. I rarely do this, so I already had an odd feeling. I got a drink of water and decided to read until I fell asleep again.

I went to the dresser to get my book, and I saw a woman in the mirror. I could only see her silhouette, but her hair was nicely styled and she was wearing long sleeves. We watched each other for a couple of minutes. Then I woke my fiancé.

"Dwayne, there's someone in the mirror, and it's not me!" I told him. He rolled over and asked what she wanted. I replied that she was just looking at me. Dwayne was already asleep again, and having seen ghosts before and knowing that this one meant no harm, I decided to bid the woman in the mirror good night and go back to sleep myself.

On Monday afternoon, Dwayne told me his Aunt Mary had died on Friday. He asked me to describe the woman I had seen. I told him about her clothes and how she wore her hair up with loose curls on the sides. She was a little larger than I but almost the same height. Dwayne told me that I had just described his aunt.

I believe his aunt wanted to see the woman he had decided to marry, since he is the baby of the family.

So, Aunt Mary, it was nice to meet you. You can rest assured that I love Dwayne, and I will take good care of him.

Joyce Doran
Fort Worth, Texas
April 1999

The Gift in the Highboy

My mother and I always were extremely close, though we were separated by thousands of miles at the time of her death. My parents Charles and Tekla Sand were then living in Milwaukee, Wisconsin, and I was in Denver, Colorado.

One of the interests Mother and I shared was the occult. She often told me her own mother had returned after death and helped her find a lost object. She promised that she would try to give me some proof of survival after her own death.

On April 7, 1971, I had a strange dream of walking down a crowded street in an unfamiliar city when suddenly the black-cloaked skeletal figure of death appeared and beckoned me toward him. I began to scream, and awakened still screaming and utterly terrified. I was afraid the dream was a bad omen, that some tragedy would befall one of my children. I did not think it related to my mother. She had had surgery during the winter but she now seemed to be recuperating nicely.

When nothing unusual had happened after a week or more I half forgot the dream. Then on the morning of April 23 it seemed everything went wrong. A bookcase fell over—right on top of my two-year-old son. By some miracle he wasn't injured, but a lovely glass wine carafe Mother had given me was broken.

Shortly after this incident the feeling of "wrongness" that had spoiled the whole morning seemed to lift. I felt light and happy the rest of the day. I was totally unprepared for my brother's call late in the afternoon to tell me Mother had died. Her death had occurred just about the time of the morning that my bookcase had fallen over.

When I returned to Milwaukee for the funeral, my father asked me to go through Mother's things and sort out what could be given away. I had completed this sad task and was standing in their bedroom for a moment, gathering strength for other tasks that awaited me, when suddenly my father's old-fashioned, heavy highboy began to shake violently. I had not looked into this chest of drawers since it contained only my father's things. But the shaking led me to open one of the lower drawers. In it I found a lovely little blue purse. I gathered that Mother purchased it for my daughter's birthday that was to come soon. I believe my mother chose this way and this reason—so similar to what my grandmother did for her—to prove to me that there is life after death.

Sue Deutsch
Milwaukee, Wisconsin
May 1976

Father Told Me

When I was twelve years old, my father, Paul Walker, passed away after being ill for many months. The first night after his death in October 1941, my mother suggested I sleep with her. She did not want to be alone and I, too, felt the need of companionship and comfort.

After Mother finally had fallen asleep, I lay staring into the darkness, trying to understand what had happened, and why.

Suddenly I felt the presence of my father so strongly I sat up. He was standing at the foot of the bed. He smiled and said, "Don't let your mother cry. Make her understand I am much better off where I am now. I have no more pain, and although I no longer will be with you physically, I shall watch over you as long as you need me."

I started to get out of bed but he held up his hand and said, "No, you cannot touch me. Just know that I am here. Help your Mother to understand."

I lay back down and fell asleep. At the funeral, and later, as the casket was lowered into the grave at Grangeville, Idaho, I watched friends and relatives crying. I wanted to say, "Don't cry, he isn't down there. He's right here!"

Later that fall, when I rode home from school one day on my bicycle, I saw my father sitting in a rocking chair on the front porch. I jumped from the bicycle and started to run toward him. Once more he raised his hand and said, "No, you cannot touch me. Do not try; it would only disappoint you and make you sad. I'm just visiting a few moments."

He smiled and was gone.

During the next eighteen years I grew up, got married, and had three children. My father helped me overcome many problems during these years, and when I would feel a little sad because he never had met the fine man I married, nor seen his only grandchildren, I would feel him near, and he would whisper, "I know. I see them."

In January 1961, my mother visited us unexpectedly because she "had a feeling" she must see me right away. One evening we talked about Dad, as she was thinking sadly of all the things she could have done to make his life a little easier and more pleasant.

As I had done many times over the years, I assured her she had made him happy and in no way could she have changed things. Finally, I told of seeing him and the words he had said to me. To my surprise she did not disbelieve me. She wiped away her tears and said she felt relieved and happy.

That night I again lay thinking long after everyone was asleep. Suddenly there was an urgent rustling in the room, and someone shook me. Frightened, I sat up. There was my father!

He said, "You can't go to sleep yet! I must tell you—I cannot stay any longer; I must go now. I have other work to do, and my work here is finished. I love all of you, but I must go on!"

With that, there was a blinding white flash, which turned to sky-blue, and he was gone.

He had stayed with us, helping us all the years we needed him. I do not know what "work" he has yet to do, but I do know there is life after death. My father told me.

Joan L. Matthews
Garden Grove, California
December 1964

Grandfather Remembered

As a child I lived with my grandparents a great deal of the time and I loved them very much. One evening I happened to ask my grandfather, John Albert Smith, "What will I do when you and Grandma die?"

He replied, "Don't worry, child. We will watch over you always."

They both passed away before I was married, but life went on as usual. In 1939 my husband and I were living in an old, four-room house in West Liberty, Iowa. The kitchen was heated by an old wood and coal range, with the stove pipe going up through the first floor to a chimney in the upstairs hallway. My husband, Walter, would get up first, build the fire, fix his breakfast, and leave for work before 6:30 A.M.

One winter morning I heard him go downstairs, shake up the stove, and slam the door on his way out. Before going back to sleep I glanced over toward the crib to see if the baby was covered. There stood my grandfather.

He was dressed in his usual gray shirt and bib overalls. He was clean-shaven except for his thick gray mustache. He smiled as he started toward my bed.

Terrified and trembling like a leaf, I yanked the covers over my head.

Soon I felt someone shake my shoulder in the same way Grandfather used to shake it. Then I heard Grandfather's voice saying, "Come on, girl. It's time to get up." He spoke in Czech, a language I had not used in years.

I was so frightened I could hardly breathe, but after a while I became brave enough to peek out. No one was there.

I jumped out of bed and hurried downstairs, where I discovered a dangerous situation. The top of the stove was red hot and the stove pipe was red almost to the floor. In a few more minutes it would have caught fire. Had I slept as long as usual that morning the baby and I would have been trapped upstairs.

That was the only time my husband forgot to close the draft before leaving for work. But Grandfather did not forget, and he came to take care of me as he had promised.

Louise Baldwin
Davenport, Iowa
February 1965

Grandmother's Spinet

I never thought much about the hereafter until the death of my grandmother Bessie Donovan. She had been a strong woman, highly intelligent, and had raised a family of six children entirely on her own after the death of her husband Ed. When her children were grown they each went their own way and Grandmother was left alone. As she grew older and couldn't get around very well, Grandmother often called on me for help. I worshiped her and enjoyed doing the small things she asked of me.

One day in June 1970 she called me and said she wanted me to have her spinet piano and I was to take it right away. She insisted that I take it before she died, for she felt her children would not remember it was to be given to me.

"They would only take it and sell it and I'd never get to play it again," she said.

My twelve-year-old daughter Angela and I both play the piano well and one or the other of us often played for Grandmother in her home. I hated to move the piano but Grandmother insisted she knew best.

Then suddenly Grandmother died, three days after we moved the piano.

One morning a few months after her death I woke up about four o'clock thinking I heard someone playing "The Old Rugged Cross" on the piano. I got out of bed quickly and fumbled my way to the dark front room. Without turning on a light, I went to the piano and touched the keys. They felt warm. Just then Angela came in.

"Mother, the hymn sounded lovely, but what are you doing up so early?"

I had wondered if I had been dreaming but when Angela spoke I suddenly understood what Grandmother meant when she said, "They would only sell it and I'd never get to play it again."

Betty Arnold
Oklahoma City, Oklahoma
May 1974

The Trunk

Over the years, I reminded Dad of a pact we had made that whoever died first was to contact the other. On December

23, 1983, my brother Jack called from Oklahoma to tell me Dad had died. We had blizzards at home and in Oklahoma, so I did not go to the funeral.

That night, I was playing cards with some friends of mine, Esther and Lou, when my cordless phone dialed itself. Esther and Lou were frightened, but I said Dad was letting me know that he could hear and see. (He had been blind for twenty years and had recently lost his hearing.)

The next morning the phone dialed itself twice, before two other witnesses. They said it was a malfunction or that someone was using my wavelength to place long-distance calls. I reported this to the phone company, but no additional calls had been made.

Because of the weather, Dad's funeral was not held until after the holidays. The day of the funeral, my phone rang frantically. Somehow, I sensed Dad was shouting to me: "Get the money out of the trunk. It is in plastic in my brown suit."

I called Jack and he told me that the Salvation Army was to pick up the trunk as soon as the weather cleared. I told Jack about Dad's message. There was dead silence. Awestruck, he said, "My God, I forgot all about that."

When he could talk coherently, he explained that when Dad went into the rest home at age ninety, he was upset because he had only a little money each month, so Jack gave him seventy-five dollars. Jack said he watched Dad wrap the money in plastic and put it in the inside pocket of his suit and lock it in the trunk.

He took the money from the trunk. My phone never dialed itself again.

Gertrude Houck
Longmont, Colorado
September 1994

Great-Grandma's Bed

In 1975, I was six years old and living in Cebu City, the Philippines. My great-grandma, Beneta Romero, was blind and very ill. She lived with my family, and her bed was in the kitchen so we could easily take care of her. She always wished that she had been able to see my youngest brother, Edwin Villanueva Pepino, who was three, since she had become blind before he was born.

One night my uncle Benjamin Villanueva Pepino, my aunt Lorna Pepino, and I were preparing our dinner and telling jokes with Great-Grandma as we always did. I was the first to notice that Great-Grandma was not responding to our jokes. She was not breathing, only lying very still in her bed. I told my uncle that Great-Grandma was dead, but he didn't believe me until he checked for himself.

The morning after Great-Grandma's funeral, my brother Edwin was found sleeping in her bed. I asked him what he was doing in her bed, and he told me that Great-Grandma had come into his room and carried him to her bed.

This happened for three nights in a row, until we went to Great-Grandma's grave and prayed for her soul to rest in peace. Edwin never did return to Great-grandma's bed. He slept peacefully in his own room.

We believe Great-Grandma could finally see Edwin after she passed away.

Rowena Dehnke
Whitehall, Wisconsin
September 1994

The Shaking Bed

My maternal grandfather enjoyed playing the guitar and the mandolin. As his family grew, he built them a larger home with his own two hands. He was always a self-reliant, independent sort. When he developed heart trouble, he ended his own life in a bout of depression. I was about seven or eight years old at the time of his death.

When I reached my mid-twenties, after a hitch in Uncle Sam's army, I had occasion to stay with my grandmother for a short time in the home built by my grandfather. There was a large picture window in the living room that looked out upon the world. My grandfather had a swivel rocker placed in front of the window. This was the only chair he used in the living room. When I came to stay with my grandmother, the old swivel rocker had been replaced with an upholstered recliner, which sat pretty much in the same spot where Grandpa used to sit.

Often in the evening after work, I would sit in the recliner and practice playing my guitar. Sometimes when I played better than usual, I would feel someone enter the room and watch me, yet I seemed to be alone. I just figured it was Grandpa, and continued to play some of the older tunes I had learned until I tired of playing, or my fingers started to get sore. It was then that I would set the guitar aside and kick back in the recliner. More often than not, I would soon feel a cold pressure on my lap as if someone were sitting down on me. The coldness would go through my body and then it would feel as if I were sitting on someone's lap instead of the chair. I assumed that I was again sitting on Grandpa's lap as I did when I was a child.

The room I slept in was the master bedroom. As a young, single man, recently turned civilian, I enjoyed visiting the local taverns on Friday and Saturday nights. My grandmother, a devout Christian, very much disapproved of this behavior, and I guess Grandpa did too. Whenever I came home late (anytime after ten o'clock was late to Grandma), and had even two drinks after work, the bed would begin to shake just as I was about to fall asleep. I'd snap awake, fully alert, and it would stop. Then again, just as I would begin to doze off, the bed would begin shaking a second time.

Finally, I learned that if I said out loud, "Grandpa, I really need to get my sleep as I have to go to work in the morning; you know how a working man needs his rest," the bed would not shake anymore, and I could sleep until morning. But this worked only if I did indeed have to work the following day. If not, the bed would shake me awake up to ten or twelve times during the night.

One time, I really had too much to drink. I arrived home after closing the bars down, and went straight to bed. Before dropping off to sleep, the bed felt as if it were spinning. Knowing that I was going to get sick, I got up and headed for the bathroom. I had left the bedroom door open, as it was winter, to allow the heat to enter my room. It was dark, and not wanting to disturb Grandma down the hall, I didn't bother with a light. I walked smack into the closed bedroom door! I opened the door and headed for the bathroom.

When I returned, I bumped into the closed bedroom door again! I got into my bed, and it began to shake more violently than ever as soon as I laid down. I sat up, and the shaking stopped. I could see Grandpa standing at the foot of the bed, arms crossed, watching me. I said, "Grandpa, I've had too much to drink tonight and I'm sorry to be coming home drunk. I've had a lot on my mind lately, and I tried to drink it all away. That didn't work, and this will never happen again." (And it didn't.)

It was then that I saw him uncross his arms and smile at me, shake his head, and walk out of the room. I was able to sleep peacefully the rest of the night, and that was the last time I ever actually saw him.

One day I asked Grandma if she had ever felt Grandpa's presence. "Many times," she said. But she especially noticed that he was near when she laid down on the sofa to take a nap. It was then that she felt invisible fingers combing through her hair, and heard Grandpa's voice softly calling her name. She said that she knew that he was always watching over her, and that he was just waiting until it was time for her to join him so that they would be together again.

Grandma passed on two years ago, so I guess they are together again now.

Grandma—and Grandpa too, I guess—finally accepted that I would have a few drinks once in a while. Grandma even said that according to the Bible and Grandpa a little bit of wine or whiskey was actually good for a person. So as long as I stayed away from beer, and limited my whiskey to five drinks or less, I could get a restful sleep. But if I even had a slight buzz when I returned home, Grandpa would keep me awake half the night shaking the bed!

Kevin Gardner
Clay City, Indiana
June 2000

Promise Made and Kept

My father-in-law, Elmer Clifford, was a man of strong character. He was always occupied but never too busy to repair a broken toy for his grandchildren or a piece of furniture for me. The noise associated with his work kept us always aware of Pop's presence.

We lived on a remote ranch seven miles southeast of Custer, South Dakota, our homes separated by a wooded hill. During the summer of 1958 Pop added a lovely room to his house. Perhaps he saw the envy in my eyes as I watched his house grow.

"When harvest is over I'll build a dining room on your kitchen," he promised "You'll have it for Christmas."

Whatever Pop promised was a certainty. I made curtains and selected furnishings from the catalog . . . but Pop didn't live to fulfill his promise. He was fatally injured in a tractor accident on July 18, 1958, and died six days later in Lutheran Hospital, Hot Springs, South Dakota.

Soon after his funeral the pounding began. I was transplanting lilacs when I heard the steady beat of hammer on nail coming from the direction of Pop's buildings. I dropped the shovel and hurried to investigate. The pounding stopped abruptly as I reached the gate that divided the property. The buildings were in full view twenty-five feet beyond the gate. I searched the premises and found nothing disturbed.

Nevertheless, the pounding continued, day after day. Then I began to notice the horses pastured near Pop's place were acting strangely. They would stare toward his house, snorting and shying, then bolt to the far end of the pasture where they kept a nervous watch on the buildings. I searched again for a possible intruder. A few days later my son Rhett and daughter Patty came running into the house, breathless and obviously frightened.

"What is that pounding up at Pop's?" Patty demanded.

"There isn't anyone there," Rhett added, awe softening his voice.

Now I couldn't blame the pounding on my own overactive imagination.

"I think Pop is trying to tell us something," I said.

That evening we told my husband Walter what we had heard. I insisted that he move Pop's new room and attach it to our kitchen. It would be the same as if Pop had added the dining room for us.

Once the project began the mysterious pounding stopped. Christmas dinner was served in the new dining room. Pop's promise was fulfilled and his spirit set free of earthly commitment.

Mecia Clifford
Custer, South Dakota
October 1969

Children and Ghosts
Spiritual Experiences of Young People

Do children have a special affinity for spiritual communication? Or are they simply more gullible, imaginative, and prone to misinterpretations?

The skeptical view is harder to sustain when one considers the following stories. This chapter features the experiences of young people—many of which were also witnessed by adults, or in which information is given to the children involved that could not have been obtained by normal means. Perhaps children really are more attuned to the world beyond than adults.

An Angel for Lauryn

Marlene and I went everywhere together. We were "Sis" and "Sissy" to everybody who knew us. We were inseparable. Our only differences were that she was a gorgeous blonde with a killer smile and I was more of an average-looking girl, so we were not easily confused with each other. She always talked of fixing me up with her brother Tom, who was away in the navy. She would wave his picture in front of my face and tease me that he was the guy I should be with.

Marlene was murdered by her boyfriend in July 1978. When I heard the news I was so shocked I couldn't even think. I felt as if my right arm had been cut off. It was the first time in my life anyone so close to me had been taken away. I was all of nineteen. Marlene had just turned twenty in February. I couldn't stand not being able to talk to her, to ride to work with her, to be with her. I prayed for her daily.

Soon I met Marlene's brother Tom, just back from his tour in the navy. I fell head over heels in love with him on our first date and married him three months later. I knew Marlene was always with us and I could still feel her presence in everything we did. We both did. She and Tom had been very close and we talked about her often.

Four years later, we had a baby girl of our own and named her Lauryn Marlene. She had my dark hair, but she had her aunt's killer smile. When she smiled and laughed, all we could think of was how much she looked and acted like Marlene.

One night when Lauryn was three, I nudged Tom about 2:00 A.M. and told him to listen. I could hear her talking in her room as if she were speaking to someone.

We looked around the corner of her door, and there was Lauryn sitting straight up in bed talking and laughing, acting as if she were carrying on a regular conversation with someone. She saw us looking at her then and turned and said, "Mama, Daddy, what are you doing?"

Tom walked past me into the room and knelt down by Lauryn's bed. I stood in the doorway and checked the thermostat on the wall. It seemed to be unusually cooler in her room than in the rest of the house.

Lauryn, illuminated only by the night-light in her bedroom, looked at her daddy and matter-of-factly said, "I'm talking to the lady in the corner by my window."

Tom looked at her and then turned to me, and I said, "What?" Tom looked back at Lauryn and reached for her little hand. "Really, Bean-Bean, what does she look like, 'cause Mommy and I can't see her."

Lauryn looked over to the corner by the window and laughed a little. "They said they can't see you." She paused a minute as if somebody had said something back to her and then she looked back at us both. "She said you guys are funny."

As calmly as ever, Tom again asked Lauryn to tell us what she was seeing. I just stood in the doorway unable to speak, both scared and fascinated at the same time.

I knew Lauryn was not talking in her sleep. She was wide awake, at ease, and not scared at all. She looked at her daddy and smiled. "She has yellow hair and it's short like mine. She's wearing a pretty white and pink dress and she's very nice. She said she is keeping an eye on me."

Tom pushed her further. "What's her name?" I heard his voice crack and I felt a tear slide down my cheek. We both had a pretty good idea who she was talking to.

Lauryn just looked at her daddy and smiled. "Her name is My Angel."

I turned and ran for my bedroom. Was my daughter seeing a ghost? We had talked about her Aunt Marlene to her many times, but the few pictures that I had of her aunt I had put away over the past few years because they were still painful for Tom and I both to look at. I went to the closet and got them out.

When I came back to her room, Tom had switched the light on and was sitting on the bed with Lauryn. Lauryn said, "My Angel said she had to go for now." Tom was trying to get her to settle down and go back to sleep.

I sat on the bed next to them and held out a framed eight-by-ten picture of Marlene. It was just a candid shot of her face that I had blown up after she died. Lauryn had never seen this picture.

"Is this your angel, baby?"

She sat back up a minute and smiled, looking at the picture. "Yep, that is my angel that's keeping her eye on me." She smiled.

Tom and I just looked at each other and he was smiling. He winked at me. We got her settled back down, kissed her good night, and waited until she fell asleep before leaving the room.

We went back to our room together, not saying anything. We both lay in bed and couldn't sleep. We held each other and were in awe of the entire situation. Finally, in the dark I heard myself asking my husband, "Do you think it really was Sissy in Lauryn's room tonight?"

There was no doubt in his mind whatsoever. "Yep, I know it was."

I tell Lauryn every day how much she looks like her aunt, and I tell Marlene how much I miss her. I thank Marlene for keeping an eye on Lauryn when I can't be there. She is the best of both of us combined.

Caryn M. Suarez
Jacksonville, Florida
November 1999

I Talked to the Lady

When I was a child we lived in Cottage Grove, Oregon, and for three of those years, between 1912 and 1915, I was considered an inveterate liar. If I was sent to the store—a fifteen-minute trip—I would be gone an hour, even if Mom had said to hurry back.

Mom's first question always was, "Where have you been?"

And my answer was always the same, "Talking to a lady."

Mom would take a deep breath and say, "I saw you standing on the corner. There was no one with you. Why can't you tell the truth?"

I was telling the truth! Several times a week I talked with this lady. Her greeting was always the same, "How are you,

Margit?" We talked of school, play, and people—some of whom I knew or had heard Mom speak of; others were completely unfamiliar.

Clothes weren't important to me then, but I noticed the lady wore a dust cap, a jabot with a gold pin, and the whitest of aprons. When conversation began to lag she would blow me a kiss, and I would hurry home to a lecture on procrastination.

The last time I saw the lady I was in a dither to get home and told her why. She walked with me as far as the alley. She said, "I love you and any time I can help, think hard of Margit O'Brien." She put her hand on my shoulder, gave me a feather-light kiss on the cheek, and I hurried home.

Mom was at the door ready to step outside when I reached for the knob. Her usually rosy cheeks were paper-white. "Is that the lady you talk to?" she asked.

"Yes," I answered, "and sometimes she tells me about people you know."

Mom had beautiful curly auburn hair and I thought of something the lady had told me. So I asked, "Mom, did you ever cut off all your hair, clear to your head, and did your mom call you John L. Sullivan?"

The color flooded back into Mom's face and neck as she answered, "I sure did, and they called me John L. until my hair grew out, but . . ."

"She told me you did!" I said.

Mom sat down in the nearest chair, shook her head and said, "I know, I know; that lady was my grandmother, but she passed on before you were born. You were named for her."

My veracity wasn't questioned after that, although the incident was never mentioned again. Nor have I ever seen the lady again. Still, I have felt her protective presence when I find myself in tight spots.

Margit Ryan
North Bend, Oregon
August 1976

Southern Comfort

If ever you've been to a funeral in the Deep South on a hot summer day, you will not forget it. The pungent smell of glads, mums, and carnations in a small country church will haunt you always. I attended many of these services when I was a girl in Rossville, Georgia, but one stands out in my mind. It was my great-aunt's funeral in 1950, when I was only eight years old.

In those days the deceased were kept at home until the services at the church. Several little friends and I were playing outside when one of the girls said, "Let's go in and see Aunt Lila."

All the little girls became excited and pushed and shoved to be the first inside. I began to walk over toward my parents, for I never had seen a dead body and I was terribly frightened. Suddenly my cousin Sarah Mae Brown grabbed me and began pulling me toward the bier. I resisted, screaming and kicking, but she was too strong for me.

Before I knew it I was standing before Aunt Lila's open coffin. She was dressed in a soft lavender gown and looked serene and peaceful but I was petrified with fear. I couldn't move from the side of the coffin until finally the children pulled me outside again. I was in a state of shock for the rest of the day.

That night I was awakened by someone calling my name. Assuming it was Mother calling me, I walked down the hall to her room. Instead of Mother, Aunt Lila was lying in the bed. She motioned me to come closer. When I did, she reached for my hand and began to explain that death is nothing to fear, that it is a beautiful event in God's plan for our lives and I never should be afraid of death nor the dead.

The next morning I asked Mother if she was out of bed for any reason during the night. She told me that my younger brother Elmo had had an asthma attack and she had spent the night in his room.

Since those years long ago I have lost other dear loved ones but the words that came from Aunt Lila after her death have helped me accept death without fear.

Susan Gerstner
San Jose, California
June 1976

Impromptu Visit

In 1948, when I was ten years old, my brother Hughie Cogan was dating a girl named Nora Carter. After Hughie brought Nora to our house to meet the family, she seemed like another big sister to me.

I had three older sisters, but Nora was special because she treated me special. While my own sisters would complain to Mother when I wanted to go with them wherever they might be going, Nora always asked me to come along.

Nora lived in the town of Sciotoville, Ohio, while we lived some fifteen miles away in the tiny village of Wheelersburg. But Nora often found a way to pop in for a Sunday visit even when she didn't have a special date with my brother. I came to love Nora and was always overjoyed when she showed up on an impromptu visit.

Unfortunately, Nora came for a visit one Sunday without first getting her mother's permission. When late in the evening she called home, her mother was distraught. She came immediately and took Nora home. After that Nora was forbidden to visit us.

Six months later, in April 1949, we all were shocked and saddened when we read Nora's obituary in the newspaper. She had died of leukemia.

Shortly after Nora's death I went to live with my grandparents Mr. and Mrs. Hughie Boggs of Franklin Furnace, Ohio, for the summer. Imbued with fundamentalist religious beliefs, I worried that Nora might not have been "saved" before she died. I became obsessed with grief for her passing and concern about her welfare.

One afternoon late in the summer my grandparents and I were sitting on the porch. Grandpa was reading the Bible to us; Grandma was mending some clothing and I was sitting on the step.

Rising from her rocker, Grandma said, "I believe someone is coming up the path. We should go out to meet them."

When I looked up, I saw Nora coming up the path! "Oh, Grandma, it's Nora!" I shouted. "Don't get up. I'll go out to meet her."

I ran up to her and took her hand. "Oh, Nora, I'm so glad to see you," I said. "Please tell me where you have been."

"That's the reason I came, honey," she replied. "I wanted to tell you I've been in Heaven. I have to go back now."

Suddenly Nora was no longer there and, as if by magic, I was perched back on the porch step. Grandpa was still reading the Bible and Grandma was still sewing. Neither of them seemed to be aware of the visit which had been so real to me.

I don't know what happened that day. Perhaps I had a dream or a vision. Perhaps my subconscious solved a problem that had perplexed my young mind for nearly three months. But I like to believe that Nora actually paid me one last impromptu visit.

Shirley Armstrong
St. Petersburg, Florida
January 1983

A Fine Arrangement

I was only four years old in the spring of 1937 and didn't understand what a funeral was, but I did know everyone was going except me. I was to stay at Grandma's farm near Birch River, Manitoba, with two ladies who were preparing lunch.

When everyone had left I went looking for my grandfather, William Bradford. He had been sick all winter and usually lay on the living room couch. But he wasn't there nor in his bedroom. When I saw him leaning against the railing on the veranda I ran outside and stared at him. He didn't look old and pale and shaky anymore. Instead of the familiar pajamas he wore a suit.

"Aren't you sick anymore, Grandpa?" I asked.

"No, sweetie. Fact is, I feel very well!" He smiled. "Want to walk?"

Strolling through the barnyard we talked about the chicks and calves. We both laughed when the white mare nuzzled my hair.

Suddenly Grandpa grew serious. "You like being here on the farm with Grandma, don't you?"

"Oh, yes!" I replied. "I wish we could stay but Aunt Edith says we have to go home soon." (My parents were divorced and I lived with my aunt.)

Grandpa nodded thoughtfully. "Sweetie, I have to go away. Everyone else will leave soon and Grandma will be alone. Now think carefully. Would you rather go home with Aunt Edith or stay with Grandma?"

"I'd rather stay with Grandma," I answered quickly.

"Your cousins will be gone. There'll be no one to play with," he cautioned.

"There's the kittens and the dog," I said.

"It's all arranged then. If anyone tries to take you away, make a fuss!" He winked—and I giggled. Usually when I made a fuss, Grandpa said, "That's enough!"

We went back to the house and Grandpa said he was going to the funeral and walked down the lane.

When the family returned I tried to tell them about what Grandpa had said but I was told to hush. Grandma heard me, though, and called me aside later. When I had told my story, she smiled.

"Don't tell anyone else about this. They wouldn't understand. And don't tell anyone this either—your mother and Aunt Edith don't know it yet but you will be staying with me!"

A few days later Grandma and I waved goodbye to the last of the relatives and that was the start of our many happy years together. The incident of my talk with Grandpa on the day of the funeral was never discussed until I was about fifteen years old and Grandma asked if I remembered it. I did, of course, and I asked if she had believed me.

"Yes," she said, "because you see, early that morning your grandfather appeared at my bedside. He told me I should stay on the farm and keep you with me. There would be strong family opposition to both ideas, he said, but I was not to give in, for this would be best for both of us."

And that is how my grandfather, on the day of his own funeral, arranged our future. Grandmother and I believe it was a fine arrangement.

Marlene J. Porter
Dauphin, Manitoba, Canada
February 1974

Little Boots

Ghost stories and legends abound in America's remote mountain areas—like Little Switzerland, North Carolina, where I was born and raised. But I don't remember being much affected by the fairy tales my grandfather used to tell us around the big fireplace before bedtime. As a boy of six, thoughts of ghosts were far from my mind. However, a strange thing happened that year (1930), which to this day is still a mystery to me.

I had a playmate of my own age named Jerry Palmer who lived nearby. We were inseparable through the long summers, and when winter came we had sleds our dads had built for us. Jerry's father always had more money than mine and Jerry always had better clothing and more store-bought toys.

My father was a moonshiner and bootlegger. Corn liquor and brandy sold for 25¢ a pint or $1.50 a gallon—when he could find a buyer who had that much money. With a small and unsteady income, my father was hard put to support the family, let alone buy nice clothing and toys.

When winter came Jerry appeared in his new clothes, wool pants, shiny little boots, and a heavy corduroy coat. I wore overalls, a denim jacket, and somebody's nondescript hand-me-down shoes. I don't think I really envied all of Jerry's advantages, but I did take a shine to those little boots.

In November Jerry took sick and died within a few days. He had been an only child and his grief-stricken parents moved away, obviously to find a place where they would not be constantly reminded of their little boy. They left behind many of Jerry's belongings.

His death made me sad and lonely. After a few weeks, I thought that if I visited the scene of our many contented hours together I might recapture some of the happiness of the past, so one day I wandered down the path through the woods to Jerry's house.

I found the house open, and as any little tad would do, I went in to explore. In a cupboard near Jerry's bed I found the corduroy coat and boots I had admired. Childlike, I carried them home with me. I hung the coat on the foot of my bed and put the boots underneath, impatiently antici-pating the following day, when I would wear that warm wonderful coat and those shiny little boots.

When bedtime came I looked again at my new treasures and happily fell asleep. Sometime during the night I was awakened by the shaking of my bed. Something was mov-ing in my room! I cowered under the covers, petrified with fear. The bed stopped shaking and the room became silent as a tomb. Then I heard the footsteps—were they Jerry's footsteps in his little boots walking slowly toward the door? I also heard a dragging noise, like the little coat brushing along the floor. I couldn't see a thing but the sounds continued through the door of my room, then silence. Finally, exhausted by my awful fright I went back to sleep.

In the morning I awakened slowly, stretched, and snuggled back for another nap when suddenly the night's events flashed into my mind. I jumped up and looked at the foot of my bed. The coat was gone. I bent to peek under the bed; the boots were gone too! Dressing quickly I dashed through the house and outside. In the snow were the tracks of the little boots and marks that showed the coat had been dragged alongside.

Summoning up the whole store of my six-year-old courage, I followed the tracks—right back to the house from which I had taken the items the day before. Thoroughly frightened, I ran madly for the haven of home.

At breakfast I had no appetite and my parents knew something was wrong. They pressed me until slowly and reluctantly I told them about my terrible night. They poohpoohed my tale, until I insisted that my father come out to see the tracks in the snow.

As the sun rose higher, shedding a welcome warmth into the woods and hollows, I began to doubt my senses. It had been only a nightmare—but no, I had gone to Jerry's house and taken the things from the cupboard. Now I strode purposefully back down the path and into Jerry's house. Less assured I approached the cupboard near Jerry's bed and cautiously opened the door, dreading to find what I knew would be there—the coat on its hook and the little boots on the floor, both showing the damp evidence of the night's travels. I firmly closed the door and made my slow and thoughtful way home.

I related the final chapter of my adventure to my mother and father who answered in the fashion of hill-country folk. "Son, don't never bother with things that belong to the dead."

Fred J. Lowery
Deer Lodge, Montana
November 1967

Mom

On February 5, 1988, my husband and I were anxiously awaiting the birth of our first child. It was also the day my mother, Andrea King, passed away. She had been living with cancer for more than two years, but she badly wanted to see her first grandchild.

We lived in different states with five hundred miles between us. Because I was nine months pregnant, my mother worried that if I traveled, something would happen to me or the baby.

The morning before she died, my mother must have known the end was near. She made the family promise not to let me drive down for the funeral.

Seven months after her death, we received the first of at least two visits from Mom. It was 3:30 in the morning.

(Mom was a night owl.) I had just gotten my son to sleep. I was lying in bed awake when I heard the front door open. It was locked, but I heard no keys. Soon I heard my son's bedroom door open. A short while later it closed. Then I heard a whispered, "Carla, I love you."

I was frozen—the hair on the back of my neck stood on end. To this day I believe my mom came to see her grandson and to say goodbye to me because I was unable to come and say goodbye to her.

When our son Joey was two and a half, he was visited by my mother again. One morning he awoke with such excitement—a big smile and bright eyes. He ran to me, saying, "The lady said I was gonna get a baby sister." It was all he talked about for days.

A few weeks passed and we forgot about it, until I was looking through an old photo album with Joey on my lap. He suddenly screeched, "That's the lady. She said I was gonna get a baby sister." I was shocked to see him pointing to a picture of my mom, whom he'd never heard about!

Nothing more happened until the next spring, when we got our proof of survival with the birth of our second child: a beautiful baby girl.

Carla Hass
Montrose, Minnesota
June 1996

A Homestead Revisited

I was only ten years old, but I remember a night in November 1926 as if it were yesterday.

My father Martin Christensen had just rented the old homestead of John Hayse about ten miles east of Paris, Texas, making the negotiations with the old man's son Will. We children first saw the large white farmhouse about sundown when Mother drove us into the yard in our old buckboard. We had to eat a cold supper because the cookstove couldn't be put up until Father went to town for additional stovepipe.

The house had three bedrooms. Mother and Father slept in one, my two brothers in another, and the hired hand in the remaining bedroom. My sister Bertie Lou and I had to sleep in the front room. Here we found a huge old sandstone fireplace with a long mantel, and from this room a wide door led on to a porch, which ran almost all the way around the house. The door squeaked a little when it was opened or closed.

I had suffered poliomyelitis and during my illness I had been pretty well spoiled. For one thing I would not sleep without a lighted kerosene lamp near my bed. I'm sure this annoyed my sister but she always let me have my own way.

On our first night in the new house, we could hardly wait for morning to explore the farm. I was so excited that I couldn't sleep but I could hear Bertie Lou's even breathing. I was thinking of the fun we would have in the big barn. Of course with braces on my legs I couldn't climb but

I could watch my brothers and I felt this was almost as good as getting into the hayloft.

I tossed until my sister awakened. "Are you all right?" she asked.

"Yes, but I can't sleep."

She squeezed my hand and mumbled, "You're just excited. Go to sleep."

Just then the door to the porch seemed to open. I grabbed my sister's hand and we stared at the door. A little old man stood in the doorway. He was very thin and, of all things, he was wearing white long johns! He had white hair, a small white mustache, and a trim little goatee. We both noticed the sharp, curled-up points of his mustache.

He stood in the doorway a few seconds, then walked toward the fireplace. He was so small and the mantel so high that his hand was above his head as he reached for the ledge. He looked down into the small fire my father had set for us.

While my sister and I clung to each other, too scared to make a sound, the old man slowly turned and walked toward the foot of our bed. As he stood looking at us I thought, "He isn't really seeing us; he's looking through us!"

Now he slowly turned and surveyed the rest of the room with a rueful expression as if he were seeing it for the last time. He hesitated a few seconds more and then, with another glance at the fireplace, slowly made his way toward the door. We felt that the door opened and closed but we knew this wasn't so, for we would have heard its little squeak.

With the old man's disappearance my sister and I came alive and let out terrified screams. We both were quite hysterical and we couldn't offer a believable explanation for our state. After Mother calmed us a little we flatly refused to sleep in the front room. Mother offered to let us swap rooms with the hired man, which we did with alacrity.

The next morning of course we had to tell what had happened over and over again. We knew we had been awake for surely we couldn't have had a duplicate nightmare—or even a duplicate dream. As we looked back on the vision my sister and I agreed there was little excuse for our terror, for the little old man surely meant us no harm. He seemed only to be viewing a room he had known and loved.

The next day my father went to town for the stovepipe. He called at the local hardware store, owned by our landlord's son, Will Hayse. He found the store closed and a wreath on the door. Later in the morning he ran across Will and offered his condolences on learning that John Hayse had died the night before.

Something clicked in my father's mind. He suddenly was struck by Will Hayse's remarkable resemblance to the description we had given of the little old man: a mustache with pointed, curled-upward ends, and a goatee. Cautiously he inquired about the elder Hayse's appearance. Will volunteered the information that he bore an uncanny likeness to his father, except that his father's hair had turned white.

Now my father told Mr. Hayse about our experience of the night before and asked him to come to our farm for dinner. Bertie Lou and I were taking our afternoon nap when my father and the younger Hayse arrived. My father gently awakened us and told us to come into the parlor. Because of my braces he had to carry me. Mother was in the parlor with a stranger.

"Mary," my father said, "this is Mr. Will Hayse. He wants you and your sister to tell him what happened last night."

I hardly heard his words, for I was staring at the stranger, whose resemblance to the little old white-haired man brought back the terror of the night before. He looked much younger, with jet-black hair, mustache, and goatee, but in size, features, and bearing he seemed to be a carbon copy!

Mr. Hayse spoke first to my sister.

"Tell me, young lady, what did this old man look like?"

Bertie Lou hesitated a moment and then answered, "He looked just exactly like you, sir, but very much older—and he wore (she hesitated) a white union suit."

"Yes," I piped up, "a white union suit like Papa wears."

Before Mother could reprimand me Mr. Hayse opened a large package. As he held up its contents we all gasped. In a large frame was a picture of the little old man we had seen.

Mr. Hayse told us it was his father. Then he asked my father the time we had seen the vision and Papa said it must have been about 9:30 P.M., for we had not been in bed very long.

Will Hayse said sadly, "That was just about the time my father died—and he died in the long white underwear he always slept in during the winter months."

Mary Starr
San Luis Rey, California
October 1967

Visions

Personal Experiences of the Afterlife and Past-Life Memories

Along with reports of communication and visits from the dead, some of our readers report that they themselves have been privileged to experience the afterlife state and return to tell about it. Others give evidence supporting the concept of reincarnation, or of a "spirit world" populated by souls waiting to be born on Earth.

Both near-death experiences and past-life memories have gained much popular attention in recent years, but these experiences have a long history. Reincarnation and trips to the afterworld were familiar concepts to the ancients, and the Bible records the apostle Paul's journey in spirit to "the third Heaven." Such experiences will likely be with us as long as humanity exists.

The Three Men

Over the many years of my life, I have had many strange and wonderful experiences. But the strangest one of all has been on my mind for most of my life. It is a vivid recollection of a scene that seems to parallel my path of life. It makes me wonder—was I able to choose my path before I was born? After you read my story, you may think you did the same thing.

It seemed as if eons of time had passed when I found myself sitting on a small white bench, looking down at my feet and wondering how in the world I got there—and from where. Bewildered, I looked up and saw three men.

One of the men sat behind a small white table and opened a shiny metallic book. I watched him as he leaned over the book, placing his hand on his forehead and his elbow on the table. He started to read but never turned to another page. The second man stood behind him, leaning over his shoulder and also looking at the book. Every now and then he would look up at me and grin. I felt as if they were reading something about me.

As I sat there waiting, I looked the three guys over. The two men reading the book were dressed in old-fashioned clothing. I turned and looked to my left at the third man. He was dressed like a jockey in a white, silklike shirt. It was opened in the front, and I could see his skinny, bony chest and a few straggly hairs. As we looked at one another he gave me a haughty look, and I could tell that he was a vain and arrogant person.

Looking beyond him, I could see the barren white ground stretching out like a prairie to the horizon, merging with a light blue sky. I saw no sign of human habitation. Being curious about my surroundings, I looked up and to my right. What I saw gave me the feeling that I was in a huge eggshell. The sky looked conical, stretching up as it darkened into the blackness of infinity. The clouds that I saw did not seem to follow the contour of a round earth, but seemed to rise up from the horizon in a perpendicular manner, intermingling red and blue colors with a dull orange glow that tried to shine through.

As I sat there amazed by the wondrous sight, I heard the man at the table ask: "Are you sure this is what you want?"

I looked at him, and after a moment of thought I replied. "Yes, for I have lived many lives. Great and important as they were, I now want to experience the life of a poor man, and know the joys of fatherhood."

He gave me a skeptical smile and stood up, closing the book. "So be it," he said, and the scene faded away.

Something made me gasp for breath. I felt an icy cold fluid enter my nose. It was stinging cold, but it made me feel good, so I breathed in again and again. As I opened my eyes I saw a light gray mist about me. I saw strange dark shadows moving to and fro. Then I heard strange sounds that frightened me, so I cried. And I knew then that I was being born again into a cold and hostile world.

Somehow, I know that my conversation with those three men sent me to my destiny—a lifetime of hardships and poverty that I had chosen. As the many years passed, I often wondered about the paths that I could have taken instead, for the trials and tribulations of my life were many. I embarked on the stormy sea of matrimony and as time passed on, I knew the painful joys of fatherhood many times. As the family got bigger, the work got harder—and the paycheck seemed to get smaller.

My occupation was that of a miner. My life was often in peril. I have always wondered who could have had the power to snatch me from the jaws of death so many times. Did those three men spare my life just to see if I would keep my covenant?

Now that it has all passed by, I wonder if those three men would laugh at me if I told them it was a great and exciting trip, and I might like to try it again.

William J. Zupancic
Wilkes Barre, Pennsylvania
August 2000

Another Chance

Thirty years ago, events occurred in my young life that opened up an exciting new reality and shaped me into the successful writer and happy grandmother I am now.

On July 5, 1970, Doyle, my twenty-three-year-old husband of less than a year, was struck and killed by lightning. Grief compounded grief, as we had lost our first baby, Rosslyn, a few months prior.

A week after Doyle's funeral I was blessed with two miracles. I found myself pregnant, and Doyle's sister called to tell me she had seen his face appear in a cloudlike mist over his grave. "You better not pick my flowers!" he had chuckled with brotherly good humor as his image faded away.

Family love and support helped me through the pregnancy. However, after Kevin's birth, the joy of my new son was mixed anew with grief that Doyle was not with us.

Early one summer morning, after giving Kevin his usual bottle of formula and laying back down on my bed, I heard voices—loud voices! The next day I called a Spiritualist medium whom I had recently met. She advised me to relax and see what would happen next. She had no idea how far I would take her advice.

My opportunity came several nights later. I heard the voices and relaxed. The voices disappeared. There was a strange new sensation of hearing my heartbeat in the early morning stillness. Suddenly, I fell through a blackness. I found myself sitting up in another bed, in another house, in another world!

A dark-haired young man walked into the room. Too excited to be fearful, I asked him, "Where is Doyle?"

"At the factory," he casually replied, as though he was in the habit of seeing young women appear in his bedroom. I quickly propelled myself through his house, taking note of all possible details. The wooden floor beneath my feet seemed solid enough, yet my body moved across it as light as wind. Outside were other surprises—bright daylight, moss-covered oak trees, and deeply rutted, sandy paths.

Suddenly I stood in front of a long, square brick building that smelled of leather and hot sewing machine oil. Before I could go any farther, I lost my hold.

Darkness engulfed me; there was a sensation of falling, and I was back on my own bed. Marveling at my new experience, I stared into the early morning darkness at my clock's luminescent face. I had returned the same time I had left: 2:45 A.M.

On my next try I found Doyle. He was waiting for me among the oak trees. He looked so handsome and vibrant as he hugged me.

I no longer felt sad that we could not be together. I was blessed with one more chance to see him, to know that he and Rossyln would be okay, and to say goodbye.

Betty Harbison
Leesburg, Florida
April 2001

I've Been Here Before

In 1941, when I was seven, I often asked my mother, Lillian Lenore Van Arsdale, to take me to a house on Main Street in Belmar, New Jersey. I was drawn to this house, and thought I had lived in it before, though my mother denied it, and she wouldn't lie to me. Yet I knew its rooms and furniture, even the window drapes.

Mother was concerned, and at times angry with me as I chattered relentlessly. I even told her all about the woman living there—what she looked like, what she wore while cleaning the house, and her cooking and baking apron.

Inside the front door was a long mirror with wood carvings on the top that hung on the entrance hall wall. There were gold coat racks on either side of it, and a bench to sit on. On the right, there was a long table in the dining room.

At the table were eight dark, wooden chairs, with big, high backs and blue cloth seats. Only the two chairs at the ends of the table had arms on them. A picture of three horses' heads hung on the left wall. I will never forget it. On the same wall were big gas lights, one on each side of the picture, and one on either side of the two windows on the right wall, overlooking the front porch.

I described the tablecloth—white lace, with the same blue cloth under it as on the chairs. A tall, dark wood and glass china closet was on the longest wall. In it were many pretty blue dishes and blue water glasses with long stems.

There were three bedrooms upstairs. The first room on the left was the biggest, containing a bed as high as my shoulders. The headboard almost reached the ceiling, and was carved with pictures of flowers, baskets and ribbons.

On this bed was a white bedspread I often described to my mother, but she wouldn't believe me. She said I had never ever been inside. When I cried for the umpteenth time, Mother took me by the hand, walked right up to the front door, and rang the bell.

A pretty woman answered the door, and I was sure I had seen her before. I knew the ring on her hand, and the apron she wore was as I described. I stood still and held my breath. She bade us come in.

While she and my mother talked in a hushed tones, my eyes roamed around the entrance hall and into the dining room. When we went in, everything was as I had described, before we entered each room. My mom was surprised, but the lady was shocked and had tears in her eyes. She hugged me tightly for a long time. Mom thanked her, and was glad that I was satisfied. I was happy that Mom finally believed me. My compelling urge was gone.

One day I heard Mom telling my aunt Emma Gifford that a five-year-old girl who had lived in that house died of scarlet fever on May 23, 1934, the year I was born. After that we never talked about it. Mother said I was not to ask to go there again.

I never did. I then believed that I had known the little girl very well, but as I grew older, I realized this was not so. I remember more things about her and the house when I see blue glasses or white lace tablecloths. Could I really have been her, keeping some of her memories?

Jean Brown
New Underwood, South Dakota
February 1994

I Remember Death

After I had several ESP experiences, I began to question my own sanity. Friends with whom I spoke advised me to see a psychologist, so I wrote to A. M. Cooper, Ph.D., a professor of psychology at California State University at Fresno.

On more than half a dozen occasions I had experienced trancelike states in which floodlights, vivid colors, and, sometimes, faces of the deceased appeared. Dr. Cooper declared that I was a "very fortunate man . . . that such experiences are given to few . . . perhaps only to those who are truly receptive to them. In this sense these experiences are abnormal—above that which is considered the norm." He further stated in a letter that great philosophers, scientists, Nobel laureates, poets, and writers had shared these experiences, and likened reporting them to trying to explain the color "red" to a blind man.

Further conversations with the doctor on the telephone led me to search further back into my life for unusual experiences. When I was twelve years old, six months after the death of my mother in 1921, I was still living with my older brother Archibald in Bauxite, Arkansas. When I became ill and had to have a tonsillectomy, my brother (not knowing better) advised me to eat all I could beforehand because I would not be able to eat for several days afterward. When I had the operations, the ether the doctors used to put me to sleep caused me to vomit, and I literally choked to death.

I floated out of my body and watched from above as the doctor and nurse worked frantically to unclog my throat. I then drifted up through the ceiling and joined other souls circling the earth.

I awoke on the operating table and was sent home that same evening, but I was told later that I had been clinically dead for about twenty minutes.

Since then I have encountered spirit beings, lights, and other unusual phenomena. I have been informed in dreams of coming events, like marriages and deaths. I wonder if my mingling with the spirits on that day six and a half decades ago opened the door to extraordinary experiences later in life.

> *Bruce A. Jones*
> *Sheridan, Arkansas*
> *February 1986*

Flight of the Soul

I became proficient in palmistry during my childhood, because my mother had a whole library on the subject. Many years later, when I was in the Sunset Heights (tuberculosis) Sanitarium in Asheville, North Carolina, I was constantly beseiged by patients begging, "Please tell my fortune." I only spoke of happy events, until Dr. Paul H. Ringer told me to tell the truth as I saw it.

When Mary Johnson, a lovely girl, was about to be released in 1934, I told Dr. Ringer that her life line ended abruptly, and that she did not have long to live. "This time you are wrong," he declared.

That night, nurse Frances Anne Jones told me that Mary had developed an intestinal obstruction and needed hospital treatment. I went to sleep about midnight, but three hours later I had a weird experience.

Mary Johnson appeared before me, and she was very agitated. I did not realize exactly what had happened to her, but somehow I knew she was dead. "You must not stay here," I said. "You will be very unhappy. No one will see you at all."

"But I am afraid," she cried. "I am afraid to go away alone."

"I will go with you," I said urgently. "Come, we must go now."

I took her hand, and at a terrific speed we seemed to whiz through the dark night toward a beautiful light. Suddenly, I felt a tug. I gasped, "I'll have to go back. You are all right now. But I can't get into my body again if I go any further."

Early the next morning Frances Anne came into my room. Before she could speak, I said, "Don't say a word. I know that Mary is dead, that she died about three o'clock."

Frances Anne gasped, "How did you know?"

Laura Hearne
Asheville, North Carolina
February 1965

My Reincarnated Son

I have seen myself in parts of two former lives and also have glimpsed the progress of someone very dear to me in a past age. In one flashback I saw myself clearly; my home was a small East Indian village near a river. My name was Saldena and I was the mother of two children, a small girl and a boy of seven whose name I do not know.

The villagers were fleeing from a band of marauders bent on ransacking and destroying the village. We were in a small, overcrowded skiff in the wake of two other boats when one of the men shouted, "The boat is sinking! Throw the children overboard."

My son was near the boat-side, holding his sister's hand, when someone pushed him roughly and he fell into the turbulent water. He clutched wildly for my hand and the look of horror in his eyes will haunt me always.

Desperately I tried to leap in after him but someone pinned my arms behind me and in the agony of that moment I lost consciousness and can recall nothing more of that incarnation. However, I attribute an unreasonable dread of water in this life to the memory of that heart-breaking experience.

The amazing part is that in this life I have seen my son. One day in 1945 as I drove through a crowded section of El Paso, Texas, I suddenly noticed a boy standing on the curb. He was about seventeen. Without thinking, I turned the car in to the curb and the boy turned a tragic face to me. His large blue eyes looked into mine and suddenly lit up as if in recognition. My eyes filled to overflowing, as did his. Reaching through the car window he clutched my hand exactly as he had done so briefly and so long ago before he had gone down in that brown, churning river. His chin trembled as he looked deep into my eyes and said, "I love you." Then we both knew.

"Will you go to my home and ask my mother to show you my paintings?" he asked. "I want you to see them."

I told him I would gladly do so and he gave me an address far down in the cheaper district of town. When I knocked at the door a frail, harassed woman opened it. I told her that her son had asked me to see his paintings. Her face flushed and she reluctantly invited me in. There were five pictures on the walls, and I was startled to find that all were scenes of Indian rivers, villages, holy men, and so on.

"Joe and his paintings make me sick," said his mother. I was surprised and hurt. "I'm so disgusted with that boy," she continued, studying me curiously. "He's moody; he's a drunkard and a total stranger to me. I've never understood him and never will. Those silly paintings—where he gets such ideas is beyond me. He never copies anything—he just paints them. I hate them but he loves them, and so I just leave them alone and stay out of his room."

Had there been any doubt in my mind as to Joe's former identity it was dispelled when I gazed at a face in one of his portraits. It was an exact likeness of his father of long ago.

I could not explain to Joe's mother that I believed him to be my son in a past life, and because she regarded me with distrust I never have contacted him since.

Miriam Teel Clarke
Farmington, New Mexico
June 1954

Up the Wide Staircase

Searing pain told me my baby and I were in serious trouble as I lay in the delivery room in Red Bank (New Jersey) Riverview Hospital on March 1, 1959. Over and over I screamed, "Please save my baby!" Then, although the pain hadn't stopped, I saw the hospital personnel rushing my precious new son to an incubator.

Still torn by merciless pain I heard my obstetrician, Dr. Berman, say, "Oh, no!" Suddenly my head seemed to fall backward and with a snapping sound I was all at once completely free—no pain, no tears, no worry.

I hovered in an upper corner of the delivery room, watching and listening as the doctor and three nurses struggled to revive the body that I knew was mine. They even sat me up on the table and ran ice up and down my back. One nurse kept trying to open my eyes and I could see her tears. I wondered why they were so excited and thought, "Don't fuss so, I love it where I am. You can have that body."

Then I floated higher, leaving the hospital scene, and in the dimness a wide staircase appeared before me. Free of all earthly connections I felt only peace as I began to ascend the stairs. In the light at the top was the glory my soul had been searching for. Then suddenly, about halfway up, I couldn't move. When I turned to see what force held me back I found myself on the street in Keyport, New Jersey, where I lived. I remembered that I was a wife and mother and felt sadness at leaving my babies.

Suddenly I was back on the stairs, once more looking up. Then I heard a soft voice saying, "You must go back. You are not ready. Go back, go back."

Going back was easy—just darkness. A day later I slowly awakened in my semiprivate room with the wonderful knowledge that my baby and I were going to be fine.

The doctor and nurses who looked at me skeptically when I described the scene in the delivery room were awestruck as they realized how detailed and accurate my recollection was; I remembered their conversations word for word.

I almost made the trip again while trying to deliver my fourth child in June 1966 but that situation was brought under control and I did not leave my body. In any case, it is a trip I do not fear. I am always being watched over and waited for.

Lois A. Walling
Pioche, Nevada
March 1976

What an Experience!

My mother was in intensive care in the hospital after a major stroke that had left her unable to talk or move. My sister and brother and I had been at her bedside for days comforting her and praying for a miracle. The only response from her was a little eye contact and tears of frustration and sorrow.

We all lived hundreds of miles away and we had to return to our jobs for fear of losing them. I drove home after telling Mother how much I loved her.

I have practiced having out-of-body experiences, so I tried it at home that night because I wanted to be near my mother. I relaxed my mind and body completely and focused on my mother's hospital room.

Suddenly I was hovering by her bedside and then flying at great speed along the beautiful blue oceanside above Highway 1. I was thoroughly enjoying this experience. I felt my mother's presence, then I saw a bright white orb racing in front of me. I knew this was Mom and I felt great joy. I raced to catch up with her.

The white orb gained speed and rushed higher and higher toward a brilliant white glowing light surrounded by mist. The orb then fell downward and I continued to pursue it.

As it fell, the orb and I went beneath the highway into what I call another dimension. We continued downward into a world of gray and black hues, similar to a photograph negative. This was astonishing to me, but suddenly I felt fear. I felt that this could be Hell.

I started back upward and the orb once again raced ahead of me. I felt gloriously happy again, and I hurried to follow the orb. The orb gained speed and shot up into the bright white light behind the mist. I continued upward. As I got closer to the white light I heard a loud and forceful voice say, "No!"

I fell downward and gently but quickly returned to my body. I looked at the clock; it was 1:38 A.M. My mother was pronounced dead at two o'clock.

I had been an atheist for years out of disillusionment with God after my mother's suffering of more than twenty years. She had been in a wheelchair with arthritis, diabetes, and other ailments.

I feel this was my mother's way of telling me there is a God and showing me the alternative to not believing in Him.

Thank you, Mom!

Valerie Bartlett
Burney, California
October 1996

Past-Life Lodge

The dream jolted me awake. Why was I dreaming of a fire in an old colonial inn? In the dream, my daughter and I were running along a third-floor verandah. It faced west and led to a staircase on the south side of the inn. We leaped to safety.

The dream's vivid details were unforgettable. Before the fire, I saw the third-floor solarium, the kitchen with racks of wooden bowls, a wood-burning stove, and a narrow circular servants' stairway. I explored the foyer with its bouquets of herbal wildflowers, saw the wide front porch with rocking chairs, and went up and down the staircase that led to the foyer.

I was standing in the bedroom with tiny roses in the wallpaper, when a man who resembled Abe Lincoln came in and hung his top hat on the clothes tree. In the dream I was about thirty years old, and was wearing a white cotton summer dress. I was in the bedroom making certain that the pitcher was filled with water and that the ceramic basin was clean. The feather bed was covered with a white cotton quilt. I recognized the colonial period, but I couldn't figure out what I was doing there.

I related the dream to family and friends. I thought it was a warning of a potential fire in my own house. I was wrong.

Four months later, my husband suggested we go to Vermont to get away from the August heat. We had never been to Vermont. When we arrived in Bennington, I was shocked to see the inn that had been in my dream. Empty rocking chairs moved to and fro on the wide front porch. There was a third-floor solarium, a verandah, and an escape stairway on the south side of the inn. Through the latched screen door of the front entrance, I could see the herbal bouquets in the foyer, and the stairway located exactly where it had been in my dream.

When the owner did not answer my knock, I went around to the kitchen entryway. Through the screen door I could see everything that had been in my dream, including the narrow circular servants' stairway. This was absolutely uncanny. How could I have dreamt these details?

Desperate to talk to someone, I went across the street to the church. That day, several people were conducting tours of the cemetery where Robert Frost was buried. I questioned the tour guide about the inn. She told me it had been used as a hospital during the American Revolution, that many presidents had stayed there, and that it was currently the private residence of a reclusive woman and her daughter. She had no knowledge of a fire at the inn. It was a historical treasure, and the owner wanted to keep it that way.

When the guide told me the name of the owner, I shook with chills. Her last name was similar to my maiden name, Burry, originally "Bury." The owner's name was Biery. In old-fashioned handwriting, *i* and *e* together were often interpreted as *u*. Research on my own Irish genealogy suggested that Biery and Bury were variations of the same ancestral name.

I departed Vermont exceeding the speed limit, totally shaken.

Caroline Totten
Canton, Ohio
November 1998

From Long Ago
Stories from the Past

When *FATE* began publication in 1948, the memories of some readers reached back through the early years of the twentieth century, and well into the nineteenth. Here is a selection of stories from the long-ago past.

Sometimes the language seems quaint, and the details of life recall vanished times: telegrams instead of e-mail; mule teams instead of tractors; horses and buggies instead of SUVs. But the evidence of afterlife survival is similar to that reported today.

Grandpa's Ghost

My maternal grandfather, the Honorable George Washington Rose, an attorney, was accidentally shot and killed by his oldest son, my uncle Oliver Steele, then twenty-two years old, in 1880. At that time my mother, the youngest of a family of four children, was seven.

From then on the sixteen-room mansion in which the family lived in Maysville, Missouri, had the reputation of being haunted by Grandpa's ghost. Many times he was heard walking about the place, and at other times he was seen by various members of the family.

One evening when I was ten years old and living in the country, about three miles southeast of Maysville, with my parents, I suddenly became violently ill with what later was diagnosed as bilious fever. My mother tried to interest me in playing dominoes to distract me from my sickness. But I started vomiting violently.

We didn't have a telephone, and my mother, alarmed, started walking with me to the nearest neighbors' house, about a quarter of a mile away up a steep hill. She wanted to telephone my father who was working away from home and was with us only on weekends. She wanted to call a doctor also. I vomited all the way up the hill along the dusty road.

When we reached the top of the hill, I looked back down at our house in the valley; it was bathed in evening sunshine. In a triangular clearing between the house, the smokehouse, and a woodpile, I saw three men. They were dressed in black; their frock coats and tall "stove-pipe" hats, which long since had gone out of fashion, were clearly visible in the brilliant sunshine. Even from a quarter of a mile away, I could see these men distinctly. They were milling around in the clearing in our backyard.

"There's Pa!" I heard my mother gasp. "Down there. Look!"

I looked at her and saw that her eyes were focused on the same distant scene.

"It's Pa and two of his associates," she exclaimed.

I've never forgotten that long-ago vision and I've often wondered at the cause of it. Was it because I was indeed near death and almost "over on the other side" that I saw these men? Or did my mother, a reputed psychic and medium, transfer this scene from her mind to mine? Were the men actually there, or simply in our minds? The fact that we both saw them must have some significance.

Cecile Word
Chicago, Illinois
July 1964

A Ghost Led Me to Water

When I was just a young man on my father's farm in Camanchie County, Texas, a good many years ago—1890 to be exact—I was plowing the fields one unusually hot day in spring and I became terribly thirsty. It was quite a ways to the house and it was about noon-time. I rested the team of mules in the shade of a grove of trees on the back end of the farm. I was tired and thirsty, and wanted a drink in the worst way. But there was no water around that I knew anything about so I decided to tough it out until it was time to quit.

I sat down and leaned against a tree, and pulled my old straw hat halfway over my eyes to keep the flies off my face. I was dozing when suddenly I heard a noise. I opened my eyes find an old man with a long white beard standing before me. I was so startled that I couldn't swallow for a moment. The funny part of it was that I could see right through this old man. But unreal as he looked, he motioned for me to get up and follow him. I did. He floated a few feet in front of me.

I never had believed in ghosts of any kind but something—perhaps curiosity—forced me to follow him through the woods. He led me to a spring that was giving forth cold, fresh water. I got down and drank until I was thoroughly refreshed. Then I got up to thank the old man, but he was gone.

I hurried to the house at quitting time and told my father about my experience. He didn't know anything about the spring. But when I described the old man to him, he said it was Old Man Warren, from whom he had bought the farm twenty years before. He said that the old man was buried now in the family plot on the farm.

Anyway, I was truly grateful for the water.

Frances B. Smith
Loma Linda, California
April 1959

Not Flesh and Blood

One day in 1914 on my way home from school I paused by a railroad track to watch a rat fighting with a crab. Gilberto Vazquez, who was a soldier and an old friend of my father's, happened by. I asked him to come and see the fight. He didn't oblige but said, "Son, this very moment I saw a soldier right where you are standing."

I was thirteen years old then. I did not attach any importance to the vision and soon forgot the matter.

After I graduated from high school in Rio Grande, Puerto Rico, my father could not afford to send me to college. I found myself out of school and unemployed.

One evening while I was sitting alone in despair on my porch I saw our friend Vazquez coming. I had not seen him for a year and hurried to meet him.

"Son," he said, "I know how you are feeling. I just came to give you my advice. The army offers lots of opportunities to young fellows like you. There is no recruiting now in my regiment but there is a vacancy in my company due to the death of a comrade. Now, if you want to get into the service go right away to the army post and ask to see Sergeant Barreto. Tell him about it. He is my top kick and a close friend."

I arrived in the post (at Fort Brooke, San Juan) by midmorning on the next day, November 8, 1921. Near a sentry box an old soldier was talking to the sentry. I asked them for Sergeant Barreto.

"I'm Sergeant Barreto," the veteran said. "What can I do for you?"

After hearing the purpose of my visit Sergeant Barreto asked, to my surprise, "Young man, is your name Padron?" I said it was, and he continued: "Vazquez told me last night about you."

As an afterthought he asked, "Are you sure it was yesterday Vazquez told you to come and see me?"

"Yes. He came to our house about 9:30 in the evening. I'm sure," I said.

The sergeant took me to the hospital for a physical exam. An hour later I was a soldier in the United States Army, in Headquarters Company 65th Infantry.

"Now, let's go and see Vazquez," the sergeant said.

We entered a room where a sentry was standing guard. There was a long table in a corner and on it lay Vazquez—dead.

"He died this morning after a brief illness," Sergeant Barreto muttered.

And so the "death of a comrade" that made a place for me in the 65th Infantry and of which Vazquez spoke to me on the evening of November 2, 1921, was Vazquez's own.

I am, today, a retired sergeant with twenty years service. I still wonder how the dying man brought his message to me. Obviously he was not of flesh and blood, yet I had not suspected this when I talked with him.

Antonio E. Padron
New York, New York
January 1963

Reappearing Ring

Throughout his college days, my great-uncle, Thomas Beaty, a geologist who traveled widely for the United States government, and his roommate, Kenneth R. Tierney, Jr., often had speculated on the existence of life after death. Uncle Tom, a skeptic, denied that there was an afterlife, while Kenneth believed firmly that there was.

Uncle Tom laughingly made a pact with Kenneth that the first to die would let the other know if there was a life after death.

Ten years after graduation, in 1911, Uncle Tom was taking a stroll in Rio de Janeiro, Brazil, when, according to my mother and grandmother, he heard his name called from the direction of some small shops. He paused, and then clearly heard his name called again. As he knew no one there well enough to be called to on the street, and as he was unable to see anyone who might have called, Uncle Tom concluded he had been mistaken and began walking again.

Once more he heard his name called, even louder than before.

This time he thought he had located the source of the voice as coming from what appeared to be a small second-hand store. He entered, and what seemed like an invisible hand took his arm and guided him to a counter of jewelry. This hand took his own, and he reached into a pile of assorted jewelry, pulling out what looked like an ordinary man's ring.

Then an electric shock ran through Uncle Tom. He recognized the ring as Kenneth's.

He examined the inner band of the ring and discovered the initials "K.R.T." Wondering what ill-fortune could have forced his friend to sell his prize possession—the ring originally had belonged to Kenneth's father, and never would Kenneth take the ring from his finger—Uncle Tom bought the ring and resolved to return it to Kenneth when he went home. Still, he thought, how odd and how lucky it was that he had discovered it the way he did.

When Uncle Tom returned to the United States, he immediately wrote to Kenneth's mother, requesting her son's address.

A few days later he received his reply: "Kenneth died six months ago of pneumonia, and until receiving your letter, I just could not bring myself to write you about it."

Mrs. Tierney added, "One more thing, when Kenneth was so ill he spoke of giving you his ring, but I am sorry to say that the ring disappeared during his illness and we have not been able to find it. I feel badly about this, for I know it was his express wish that you were to have the ring."

Uncle Tom remembered that night of graduation when a laughing young Kenneth had said to him, "Tom, do not forget our pact. If I go first, wherever you may be, somehow, some way, I will prove to you that there is another life. I will let you know there is a hereafter in a way you cannot possibly mistake. I will prove it to you."

The manner in which he received Kenneth's ring convinced Uncle Tom of the truth of his friend's belief, and he himself went on to convince many others of the existence of an afterlife. To his dying day he wore his friend's ring and throughout eternity he will wear it, for the ring was on his finger when he was buried, as he had wished it to be.

V. A. Santore
Youngstown, Ohio
April 1963

Visitation

In March 1930, I lived in Santa Barbara, California, with my father, an older sister, and a younger sister. My mother had passed away a little more than a year earlier. I was eighteen years of age and was very ill with pneumonia. I do not remember the exact date but on this particular day the doctor had come and gone.

Father, who worked nights, was in his room asleep. My oldest sister was not at home and my youngest sister had not yet returned from school. I was alone in my room, feeling terribly low and wondering if I shouldn't just give up the struggle to live.

All of a sudden I felt a peculiar thrill. I looked up and saw my mother standing at the foot of my bed, her hands resting on the wooden bed railing.

She looked exactly as I remembered her from my childhood. The gray was gone from her hair and the lines from her face. She looked much younger than when I'd last seen her. Her appearance was vivid and real. She was wearing a pale blue dress.

My first thought was that she had come to get me. I blurted out, "Oh, Mother, take me with you."

With her large, dark brown eyes fixed on mine, she shook her head and replied, "You have much to do." She repeated the sentence twice as though trying to impress it firmly on my mind. Then she was gone.

Needless to say, after this my outlook was much improved and my recovery was remarkable.

I have kept the memory of this visitation a secret all these years. Just why, I do not know. Countless others have experienced similar phenomena, and history records that such visitations occurred long before Christ. As long ago as 850 B.C., the blind poet Homer recounted the visitation of what he called a ghost: "'Tis certain man, though dead, retains part of himself; the immortal mind remains; the form subsists without the body's aid."

Marie Beckleman
Mountain Center, California
July 1964

I'll Return to Heaven

When I was two years old my dear mother died and I went to live with my papa's mother. She was good to me and taught me many things. When I was four my papa married a wonderful woman who became my loving mama.

In the winter of 1896 I contracted a serious case of pneumonia. I had terrible nosebleeds and a fever so intense that nothing seemed to bring it down. In those days small bits of cotton were tied with a short string and the cotton was dipped in a solution given us by the doctor. These cotton bits were inserted in each nostril to stop the bleeding and when dried they were pulled out and new pieces inserted. Cold cloths were put on my forehead.

My dear stepmother sat beside my bed and tended to me, wringing out a cloth from a pan of ice water on a nearby table. She was there day and night except when Papa could take her place.

One day Papa stayed home from work so that Mama could get a little rest. The doctor came every day and this day I heard him say, "If the fever doesn't come down, I don't think she'll last the day. I'll stay with you."

Just then someone knocked on the door. It was a boy asking for the doctor. He said his mother was suddenly sick and in urgent need of attention. The doctor told my folks that this woman, who lived down the block, was expecting a baby soon. He said he hoped it wasn't coming now but he would go see her and if anything happened to me before he got back to come and tell him at once. Then he left.

Mama had continued to sit with me while the doctor talked with Papa, but now Papa brought her coffee and took her place by my bed. With his beautiful voice he sang some of the nursery songs I loved. After a while Mama came back and Papa went to have his coffee.

Suddenly I had a strange feeling. All at once I floated up to the ceiling and from there looked down at myself lying on the bed. Then a force pushed me into a dark tunnel and I was afraid. I couldn't control my actions; I just floated. I saw a great light ahead, a light I'd never seen before. I wanted to reach the light. I thought it was the Heaven I'd heard about in Sunday school.

When I reached it, I felt wonderful and wanted to stay forever. A beautiful person of light came to meet me and I said, "I'm happy to be here. Are you the guardian angel I've heard about in Sunday school?"

This creature of light said, "Yes, I am your guardian angel and I'll be with you always. But you can't stay here now. You must go back, for you have a long life ahead of you and lots of work to do. You will have seven children."

Mama was hearing my side of the conversation and couldn't figure it all out but she sensed that I was near death. Suddenly I was pushed and pulled back onto the bed. I felt myself drop and looked up to see Mama crying. Papa came back and she told him what I'd said and he came over to kiss me.

I felt wonderfully well and strong. I sat up in bed, something I hadn't been able to do, and told them about my guardian angel. I pulled the strips from my nose. They were dried and my nose had stopped bleeding. My fever was gone; I was cool and comfortable.

I told Mama I wanted something to eat. "Hot milk and buttered toast," I said.

When the doctor came back he looked at me in astonishment. "This is a miracle," he declared.

Mama told him what she'd heard me saying and what I had reported to her. He laughed and said, "With seven children, she'll have her work cut out for her."

The years passed. I grew up, married a wonderful man, and had seven wonderful children: two sons and five daughters. I felt blessed. I am ninety-three years old now. Six of my children are still living. I have grandchildren, great-grandchildren, and one great-great-granddaughter. Mine is a wonderful family. With wives and husbands and children we number fifty-six.

Many friends, on hearing my story, think I imagined it. But what four-year-old could imagine such a tale? I believe I did go to Heaven, and at the end of my life I will return.

Hazel Smith
San Diego, California
January 1986

Scolding Spirit

I remember my grandmother as a darkly clad old lady who seemed always to be sitting in a hard, straight-backed chair. We were never close emotionally and seldom talked.

She died when I was twelve years old. Soon afterward I began to hear her voice. She always scolded me because I was doing something I shouldn't. This frightened me at first; but since no one else seemed to hear her I carefully kept her presence to myself. After a time I grew so accustomed to her voice I scarcely paid any attention to it.

In 1903, when I was nineteen years old, I was a student in the engineering school of Göttingen University in Germany. We spent six months in the classroom and six months in a factory practicing the theory we were supposed to have learned. One day in a factory in Kiel, Germany, I was doing routine work on a lathe. There was absolutely nothing dangerous about the work. Suddenly Grandmother began to chatter.

"Stop. Move back. Go away. Stop working."

I paid no attention but she was so persistent that I eventually shook my head and stepped back, thinking that she might then leave me alone.

Almost instantly there was a tearing sound in the air over my head. From a platform about ten feet above where I had been standing a small electric motor, used to run the belts, came plunging down. It smashed to bits on the edge of the machine where I had been working. If I had been there, I would have been killed.

Immediately Grandmother proceeded to give me one of the worst tongue-lashings about obedience I ever received.

I heard her many times after that. And you can bet that every time I was quick to obey.

Alan J. Ramm
Westfield, New York
June 1954

"Surviving" the Johnstown Flood

Aunt Mag, Mrs. John Day, of Prospect, Maryland, was out working in her garden when she saw the minister drive up and stop at her gate. As he climbed out of the buggy, she walked slowly down the path to meet him.

"How do you do, Mrs. Day," he said. "Are you very busy? I have something important that I want to tell you about Grace and your husband. Let's go onto the porch for a moment."

Aunt Mag followed him without a word. Pulling out the old rocker for him, she leaned against the post as she said, "I guess you want to tell me that Grace and John drowned yesterday in the Johnstown Flood. But I know."

"How did you hear?" the preacher asked in amazement. "The news just came in on the wire and I hurried out to tell you so you wouldn't see it in a paper first. How did you know?"

"Grace came to me last night and told me," Aunt Mag said. "She was afraid my heart wouldn't stand the shock if I read it in the papers. She told me not to worry, she was all right, and I would see her soon again. So I appreciate your coming around to tell me, but it really wasn't necessary. She told me that she was on the train when it had to stop because the bridge was washed out. She and Dad hurried off, but she forgot her umbrella and went back to get it. It was her new one. The water swept the train away and they were drowned in the flood."

Days later a relative of Mrs. Day's, Mr. Howard McGinnis, told the preacher it had happened exactly as Mrs. Day had said—exactly as Grace had told her it happened.

I also heard the story from Mr. McGinnis. But the first time I heard it was after I had seen a movie about the Johnstown Flood, which had occurred on May 31, 1889. I was telling my parents about the girl in the movie who forgot her umbrella and went back to get it.

"Why, that was your daddy's cousin! That's her picture over the piano," they told me. They also told me the story of Aunt Mag's experience. According to her picture Grace was a very attractive girl.

Marie Gouker
Lakeland, Florida
May 1965

As Grandfather Left

In April 1920, when I was fifteen years old, my maternal grandfather lay dying in a bedroom across the hall from where I was sleeping.

Grandfather, Rev. H. B. Hartzler, was then eighty, a retired bishop of the Evangelical Church and a former editor of the church paper. He had been ill for several weeks, but due to his age he was sinking fast. The doctor told my grandmother that evening as he left, "He'll go anytime now. I doubt that he'll live through the night." There was nothing more the physician could do.

That was the situation as I crawled into bed sometime after eleven o'clock. As I drifted off to sleep I heard my grandmother moving around and talking with the nurse on duty.

Suddenly I woke from a deep, dreamless sleep, my heart pounding. What awakened me I'll never know. The house was quiet, yet I was wide awake. Something impelled me to jump out of bed and go quickly to the bedroom window on the southeast side of our Lemoyne, Pennsylvania, house. As I gazed into the yard, which was bathed in bright moonlight, my attention was drawn to a slow-moving figure. My heart still pounded and I grew a bit dizzy as I recognized my grandfather.

I very well knew Grandfather lay on his deathbed in the adjoining room. But the figure in the yard was Grandpa all right, in a collarless white shirt. (He had a habit of removing the hard collar and black tie he always wore when he arrived home from the office.) His black trousers were held up by a pair of suspenders, the buckles of which seemed to glint in the moonlight.

He was bareheaded and his flowing white beard seemed sharply delineated as he paused by a small apple tree he had planted the summer before. Then he turned his face heavenward. I never will forget his expression. It was one of complete peace and joy.

Suddenly galvanized by fear I jumped back into bed and pulled the covers over my head. I still was shaking when the door to my room opened and Grandmother came in.

"Richard, Richard," she called softly, her voice breaking. "Your grandfather has just been called home to Heaven."

In a faltering voice I replied. "I know."

Richard H. Steinmetz
Camp Hill, Pennsylvania
January 1965

The Brothers' Farewell

My uncle Edmond Dawson died on August 30, 1916, a typically hot midsummer day in Cortland, New York.

In Huntington, New York, where we lived, not much was doing in my father's line of work at that time of year. My father, Leonard Dawson, was the only chiropodist in town and he had his office over a shoe store. It was a small office approached by a steep staircase. Near the top was a landing and then two more steps to the left. It was my father's custom after lunch to sit in his customer's chair facing the stairway, put his feet up on the footrest and take a little nap.

One day he wakened to see his brother coming up the last two steps and as he reached the newel post he stopped and stood with his hand resting on it. Dad was glad to see him and got up to greet him. He reached out to shake hands, saying, "How are you, Edmond?"

At the sound of Dad's voice Uncle Edmond disappeared. Shaken by this experience Dad went downstairs to ask the shoe store manager, who had been standing at the doorway, if he had seen a man come up. The manager said he had been standing there for some time and no one had entered.

One hour later my father received a telegram notifying him of his brother's death.

Dorris Hartford
Huntington Station, New York
June 1967

Dad Went to Hell

In 1926 I was a fourteen-year-old farm girl living in a back-country section of western Kentucky when I had a psychic experience that changed my family's life.

One bitterly cold February night, the sputtering log in the fireplace did little to alleviate the chill in our dilapidated house. My decision to go to bed at seven o'clock was motivated more by a need to keep warm than a yearning for sleep. There would be little sleep in our home this night. My father, Marshall Bennett, had left earlier in the afternoon for Simon's Tavern, a neighborhood roadhouse noted for bad whiskey and people of low repute. It was a rare night when someone wasn't injured in a cutting or shooting scrape in Simon's Tavern.

Dad was not a bad man. He worked hard to scratch a living out of the poor, thin soil of our hill farm. Other times he worked on neighboring farms from sun-up to sunset for fifty cents a day. He had gradually grown bitter and taken to drink, and when he was drinking he took out his frustrations on his family. Generally we didn't go to bed on nights when he was out on a binge. We would just sit and wait, dreading to hear his stumbling footsteps on the porch.

During this period a bizarre facet of Dad's nature started to emerge. This was his unreasoning and brutal treatment of cats. One afternoon he suddenly jumped up and took his gun down from the wall. "I'm gonna do a little hunting," he announced. A few minutes later we heard shotgun blasts coming from the direction of the barn. My mother Janie ran to see what the shooting was about and found the bullet-riddled bodies of several cats. "I'm wiping out this cat den," Dad declared triumphantly. He wasn't kidding. Before the week was out he had systematically slaughtered every cat on our place.

Shortly after that a beautiful marmalade tom took up at our farm. Thinking that Dad had spent his rage, I started feeding the cat and he quickly became my pet. Tragically I was wrong in thinking Dad's vendetta was over. One morning, about a month after the marmalade cat had come, I had just finished milking the cow. I always gave the cat a little warm milk in a pan I kept at the barn. That morning Dad walked in and found the cat lapping the milk. He flew into a rage.

"So this is what goes with our milk!" he stormed.

Seizing the cat by the scruff of the neck he started shaking it. The frightened animal reacted predictably by raking Dad with his hind claws. Dad cursed the cat and raised it high above his head. "No, no, please don't!" I screamed. I tried to grab his arm but I was too late. He slammed the cat against the corncrib, crushing his skull. At that moment I started to feel an intense hatred for my own father.

Through the rest of that summer and fall Dad made our lives a living hell. He drank and gambled away every penny he was able to get his hands on. Mother had strong religious roots and she tried valiantly to keep our spirits up, telling us that we were going through a trial and things would be better after we proved our faith. Secretly I longed for the time when I would be able to leave home. I couldn't understand that Dad was a sick man. To me he was the living personification of Satan.

So when I went to bed that cold February evening I fully expected that we were in for another explosion of Dad's violent temper. It usually started with his demand that we get up and prepare him a big meal.

Before turning in I lighted the kerosene lamp and set it on the bedside stand. On nights when Dad was out we always left the lights burning. I didn't go to sleep but I lay there an hour or more in deep thought. Suddenly out of the corner of my eye, I noticed that the lamp was moving, slowly sliding toward the edge of the stand as if some unseen hand were pushing it.

I reached out and moved the lamp back to the center of the stand. Immediately it started inching slowly, inexorably, toward the edge. Somewhat exasperated I returned the lamp to a safe position once again. I resolved that this would be the last time I would save the lamp. "If you fall, you fall." I said aloud. The family had been through so much anguish that I was totally apathetic about the future. If the lamp fell to the floor and set fire to the house I couldn't care less. The lamp inched toward the edge of the stand and teetered there. I closed my eyes and waited for the crash that seemed so imminent. When the crash didn't come I opened my eyes only to see that the lamp had returned to the center of the stand.

Before I had time to breathe a sigh of relief I started to feel the unmistakable presence of something or someone else in the room. Cats! The room was literally full of cats— cats sitting on the floor and on the bed, many of them my former pets. Sitting by the lamp on the bedside stand was the big marmalade Dad had so brutally killed.

Strangely I felt no fear. Indeed I felt a wonderful sense of peace and comfort, as if the cats were comforting angels reassuring me that everything was going to be all right. I reached out my hand to caress the yellow cat but my hand simply passed through the animal. Then, as suddenly as they came, the cats were gone. I immediately fell into a restful sleep.

When I awoke in the morning Dad still hadn't returned home. This had never happened before. As much as he drank he always came home when the tavern closed.

"Oh, he'll be home directly, I'm sure," Mom said and started to prepare breakfast. We didn't have long to conjecture as to Dad's whereabouts. Before Mom had breakfast on the table two men came carrying Dad home in a wagon. They had found him lying at the side of the road a little way from the tavern.

Dad was not dead but he was very ill, out of his head with fever and oblivious to everything around him. He had been suffering from a cold and exposure to the chilly night air gave him pneumonia. He lingered in a sort of never-never land between life and death for six days.

Then, on the seventh morning, he regained consciousness. He was a changed man. He told of horrible nightmares, lakes of fire, hideous tortures. He had been on a tour of hell and had returned.

Before long Dad was up and about and things immediately started to improve for us. He got a job at a tile factory and the man who owned the factory allowed us to move into a house on his property. It was rags to riches. The house had modern plumbing and Dad was finally making enough money that we could have some of the things we could previously only dream about.

I cannot explain the cats' visitation. I can only attest that they brought me comfort.

Marie Crowe (as told to Mel Tharp)
Crossville, Tennessee
May 1983

Companions

Cases of Animal Survival

Animal lovers will be pleased to discover that many reports of survival involve the return of dearly departed pets to their former owners. The afterlife is evidently not a humans-only affair.

Return of Wimpie

In June 1939, my husband and my two sons were working at a gold mine near Iowa Hills in northern California when a strange dog visited their camp. After two tentative calls the dog accepted them wholeheartedly, eating, sleeping and sharing their lives in every way, except that he refused to go down into the mine with them. They named him Wimpie.

The ore was lifted up a 350-foot shaft by a heavy steel cable that had been built to carry a load several times greater.

One morning in September the boys were about to be lowered into the pit as usual when Wimpie came tearing up, barking vigorously and intruding himself between the boys and the rim of the shaft. They paused to quiet him, surprised at this demonstration for he never before had objected to their descent.

Wimpie could not be quieted and when the boys were lowered into the shaft he howled until my husband dragged him away to the cabin.

The ore-bucket was loaded and had traveled about half-way up the shaft when suddenly the great wire cable, crystallized by age they afterward found, splintered and let its load crash down into the pit.

Had the burden been men instead of ore, Wimpie's fears would have been fully realized.

But how did he know that big cable was going to break?

With the autumn snows work at the mine was abandoned and the miners broke camp. My husband brought Wimpie home to live on our southern California ranch.

As Wimpie grew old he met with a sad accident and had to be put to sleep. He had been a regular member of the family, with the freedom of the house and it had been his delight to go from room to room greeting us all every morning.

The morning after his death I was greatly surprised when, half-waking, half-dreaming, I saw Wimpie frisking about my bedroom. He rubbed against the bed to be petted. I laid my hand on his stiff black shoulder and he leaned hard against it, just as he always had. I felt the strength and vitality in his wiry body.

"Why, Wimpie!" I exclaimed, "You are back, as well as ever."

My son came to breakfast smiling that morning. "I had such a vivid dream, Mom," he said. "I thought Wimpie came tearing to my room about daylight, just like he used to!"

We never grieved for Wimpie after that. We knew he was taking care of himself.

Ethel Bailey
La Mesa, California
July 1955

Cuppy's Hissy Fit

Cupcake was my favorite cat. There was a special bond between us, and she had set routines involving me. When I watched television, Cuppy would perch on the back of the easy chair so I could stroke her. At 10:00 P.M., her feeding time, she would find a spot in my line of vision, stare at me, and make little beeping sounds. When I returned home from my morning jog, I would rest on a boulder in my backyard. Cuppy would invariably appear, rubbing against my leg and flopping down at my feet.

But Cuppy rarely acted friendly toward anyone else. This was especially true of other cats my family adopted. Cuppy didn't appreciate my paying attention to the newcomers, and she wouldn't have anything to do with them. Her back would arch, her ears would go back, and she would growl and hiss, intimidating the intruders. We called it "Cuppy's hissy fit."

Cuppy died on April 15, 1996, after almost fourteen years as my companion. I buried her next to the boulder in our yard. We adopted other cats, but none could replace Cupcake.

One fall morning in 1998, I returned from jogging and sat down. I noticed our newest cat, Sizzle, ambling in the yard, and called him over. As Sizzle walked in front of Cuppy's grave, I jokingly introduced the two cats. Sizzle suddenly leaped back, eyes agape, and dashed away.

I could only think that Sizzle was a victim of Cuppy's latest hissy fit—from beyond the grave.

Bill Deane
Fly Creek, New York
June 1999

Twin Accidents

I was eight years old in 1949—a little girl with bright auburn pigtails just learning how to ride a bike in the quiet streets of our neighborhood in Braintree, Massachusetts. On a hot July day my girl friend Jackie and I were racing to the corner drugstore to buy a strawberry sundae. Jackie was just about there.

"Come on!" she yelled. I wanted to hurry. The pedals went round and round and the wheels wobbled wildly. I was headed directly toward a red brick wall and I just couldn't stop.

The next thing I knew I was lying on the side of the road and Jackie and an elderly man were leaning over me. Blood gushed from a small cut near my right temple.

"What happened?" I asked, trying to get up. My head felt like a squashed beanbag and I fell back hard.

"I saw the whole thing from my front window," the man said. "You hit the wall and flew over that car." He pointed toward a blue Mercury parked nearby. "Look at your bike. It's a miracle you weren't killed."

I looked. The front fender was bashed in and the wheel was twisted into a figure eight.

"I called the police. They should be here soon."

Minutes later a red ambulance arrived, and with sirens screaming it rushed me to South Shore Hospital.

"Concussion," the doctor said, placing me under observation for the next forty-eight hours.

I lay back against the pillow and thought about what my parents would say—and about Happy. Happy, my little mongrel pup with brown and white patches and a flipped-over left ear. How I loved that dog! I had lots of friends, but Happy was something else. He was the only one you could tell a secret to and know it would stay a secret. And every night he'd sleep with me.

Little did I know that he, too, had had an accident. He'd been hit by a car.

During the night I awakened to find Happy sleeping near my feet on the sterile white coverlets. Surprised, I sat up and patted him. "What're you doing here, boy? You better go home."

Lying back against the pillow I rang for the nurse. A moment later she came in with a flashlight.

"My dog is here. You'd better take him out."

A beam of light shone around the room.

"There's no dog here, honey. See?" She flicked on the light.

My eyes eagerly searched the room, finally coming to rest on the green wall clock. It was 4:15 A.M.

"But I saw him."

"You must have been dreaming," she said. She brought me a glass of water and told me to go back to sleep.

The next day when my parents came I asked, "How's my dog? How's Happy?"

The look that passed between them made me tremble.

Then Mother spoke. "Uh . . . well, honey . . . we were going to tell you last night but we didn't want to upset you. Happy was hit by a car yesterday."

"Is he . . . ?"

"He died this morning at four o'clock."

Jeanne L. Kung
Skokie, Illinois
January 1972

King Returns

During World War II, my son-in-law was hired by the Charleston Naval Shipyard. The only bad part of the job was that he would be working at night. He and my daughter wanted to live on an island, and they chose one called "John's Island." Their place was a little remote, but the community was building fast.

With four small children, they decided to get a watchdog for protection. They found a huge, beautiful German shepherd. He was named "King," which suited him well. He was kept in the fenced backyard during the day, and brought into the house at night.

The first week he was there, his barking drew everyone's attention to a large alligator on the back stoop. It took three men from a wildlife center to rope the alligator and take it away.

I was living and working in Columbia, South Carolina, and I spent my vacations with my daughter and grandchildren. I visited once about a year after they moved in. It usually took a couple hours' driving to get there, but this time I ran into storms that slowed me down and I was a little late getting there. We decided to go to bed early. We usually caught up with all the news before going to sleep.

The children were bathed and put to bed early, then I took a shower and got into my bed in a small bedroom. There was another single bed next to mine, with just enough space between the beds for a small table.

Suddenly, my bed gave a shudder, and there was King at the foot of my bed looking at me. I spoke to him, and the bed gave another shudder as he jumped over to the foot of the other bed.

Dee Dee, my daughter, came in and snapped on a light. I asked her when she had let King in.

"I didn't, Mom," she said. "I didn't tell you before because I didn't want to upset you, but King got out of the backyard and was killed by a car."

"But he just came in here and jumped onto my bed."

"Oh, he's never left, Mom—I hear him and see him often. He still protects us; he's in the children's room now."

I could understand how he could scare anyone away— he looked so real. I was glad that he decided to stay in the other room that night.

He loved his family enough to watch over them, even after his death.

Estelle Calais
Graniteville, South Carolina
May 2000

Poncho

In the summer of 1967, I was sixteen years old and I received my first puppy. It was given to me by my cousin Holly Sampson. His name was Poncho. He was two months old and he had long black hair. Although he was a mixture of husky, shepherd, and Labrador, he looked very much like a spitz with his adorable curly tail. He grew to be about the size of a shelty and was the best little buddy I ever had.

He remained with me when I grew to adulthood, and when my son Chad was old enough to play out in the yard, Poncho also adopted him for a buddy and faithful friend.

In the summer of 1977 my two children and I moved back to Thief River Falls, Minnesota, from Ozone, Arkansas. We were unable to find a rental unit that allowed pets, so we had to leave Poncho with my parents Bennie and Delores Miramontes, who lived on the edge of town and were more than willing to take him.

Winter came and went. Determined to have Poncho back with us in March, I proceeded to find a unit that allowed pets. But when I went to my parents' home, I learned that Poncho had died late in January.

I was heartbroken; so was Chad, who was eight years old. My parents tried to comfort us but I felt a loss so deep that I could not shake it for months to come.

One night the following winter I was tossing and turning in bed. I found that the only way I could get back to sleep was to kick off the blankets, since it was warmer than usual.

As I started to fall back to sleep, I felt weight on the end of the bed, as if an animal had jumped up and was lying there. I also felt soft fur on my legs. Assuming it was Tiger, our angora cat, I let my toes caress the fur as I grew more relaxed and drifted into a deep, peaceful sleep.

In the morning when I went out to pick up the mail, there sat a very patient Tiger waiting for someone to open the door after his obviously sleepless night.

From that moment on, I knew that my night visitor had been our dear Poncho coming to reassure me that everything was all right.

Dee Johnson
Thief River Falls, Minnesota
January 1984

The Phantom Cat

When we moved back to Indiana in July 1971, I rather hated to leave Pennsylvania, but once across the state line I was glad to be home again. At that time we lived in the country on a Mitchell, Indiana, rural route.

We had been away almost six months, and when we walked into our house I thought I had never seen so many cobwebs in my life. It took me all day to get rid of them. Next I discovered we had field mice. In a week of setting traps I'll bet I caught a hundred of them.

One day on the radio I heard a program called "Swap Shop" and one of the listeners calling in had a cat she wanted to give away. I put down my mop, broom, and dust rag and called the woman's number.

"She's just what I need right now—a good mouser," I told her. "I'll pick her up this afternoon."

"Now, she isn't a pretty cat," the woman said, "but she is a good mouser."

"That's all I care about," I said. I wanted that cat even if it was cross-eyed, just as long as it had mice on its menu.

Well, that afternoon I picked up the ugliest, raggediest cat I had ever seen. It was gray with a long body and tail and patchy fur.

"She may not be pretty, but if you want a cat to catch mice, she's it," the woman said, afraid I would reject this odd-looking creature.

To her surprise I thanked her and took the cat out to the car. Her name had been "Phyllis Diller" but I renamed her "Mamma," partly because of the yardful of kittens we had left behind. By the time we reached our house Mamma and I were good friends. She went into our house as if it belonged to her and I were her guest.

Mamma was everything the woman had promised—clean, neat, quiet, and a good mouser. But as all lady cats go she was nocturnal. And soon she gave us four kittens, one gray, two black, and one calico.

Even with her new family Mamma didn't break her old habits. She was a good mother during the day, but her nights were her own. She went out every night at exactly nine o'clock and returned at five every morning.

The morning the kittens were ten days old Mamma didn't come home. By noon I had given her up and started feeding four hungry babies with an eyedropper.

Every morning I had to get up at five o'clock for their feedings. One morning I went to the kitchen half-asleep and as I warmed the milk and washed the eyedropper I felt a cat rubbing against my legs. It seemed I couldn't move without this large cat getting in my way. Finally it dawned on me that no large cat lived in our house anymore. I thought that in my sleepy state I must have imagined a large cat under my feet.

The next morning after I fed the kittens, I was washing the breakfast dishes and again felt a large cat rubbing against my legs. I knew this was not imagination. It continued to happen for several weeks and I was never afraid. I felt as if an old friend were dropping in to say hello.

One afternoon we found Mamma. She had been dead a long time. We buried her in the field behind our house and I never felt the invisible cat around my legs again.

I believe Mamma had a strong motherly instinct and was watching over her kittens even after death. She used the only way she knew to say, "Thank you."

V. C. Poole
Colitic, Indiana
May 1981

Pepper

In the early 1980s I had a cat named Pepper, to whom I was very attached. I had him for three years. He was very loving and affectionate. He would always follow me and sit by me. He would sleep right at the foot of my bed and wake me every morning with a kiss on my face.

Late one Friday afternoon I was called by Martha Wickey, my neighbor, who told me she just had seen my cat Pepper get run over. I ran outside and found him lying on the road, dead but still warm.

I was heartbroken, but I got a box and started to dig a grave. I was sobbing so hard I couldn't finish the task, so my husband took over.

Later that night, when we went to bed, I heard a meow at the foot of the bed and felt light paws walking across the bed. My husband, Steve Delgadillo said, "Don't say anything, but I heard and felt your cat on the bed."

Pepper came back to say goodbye to me. My husband wasn't a believer before that, but he is now.

Cynthia Pritchett
Spring Valley, California
July 1994

Your Neighbor Shot Me!

Peg O' My Heart was a chihuahua we received from our son when she was six weeks old. Peg was more human than dog from the start, and she seemed to know what we wanted her to do. We talked to her a lot, and before long she could make her wants known. She would twist her mouth around and say, "Water," "I want to go out," or "I'm sick," very plainly.

My son grew up, my husband passed away, and so Peg and I lived alone. I talked to her all the time; she seemed to understand all that I said.

In June 1962, I promised two ladies that I would drive them to Florida. I made arrangements with Helen, the lady who cleaned my house, to take care of my Peg because they got along well together.

The evening before I was to leave for Florida, some friends dropped by and stayed quite late. As they were leaving, Peg ran out and around the house as she often did. After they left, I called Peg to come in, but she did not come. Thinking that she had come in and gone to the basement, I looked for her there, but she was nowhere to be found. I drove around the city looking for her, but without success. By this time it was four o'clock. I came home and went to bed, leaving the doors open in case she returned. I slept for two hours.

When I awoke, I called the police, the vet, and my neighbors. I gave Helen my key and some money to take care of expenses. I left for Florida, where I had an awful time, and I came back early. I continued to look for Peg for six months, and I never gave up.

Thirty-three years later, in June 1995, I awoke in the middle of the night. I thought someone had broken into my home, but when I opened my eyes, Peg was standing next to my bed. I said, "Peg, honey, what happened?"

She said, "Your neighbor shot me." I said, "What neighbor? We had nice neighbors, no one would shoot you."

She said, "I was dead before you started to look for me. He shot me, put me in a bag, and threw me in the river." Peg licked my hand and vanished. I sat there in the semi-darkness for over an hour, tears streaming down my face, hurting, but glad at last to know what had happened.

My desire was to go to that town, find those people, and tell them what I knew. But at eighty-one years of age, I couldn't even have walked the two blocks from my old house and gone down the bank and across the railroad tracks to where Peg had been put into the river.

Instead, the next morning I cut a large bunch of flowers, drove forty-nine miles, and stopped my car on the bridge just below where she went in. I tossed the flowers in, cried again, and came home. Now at least I know what happened to her.

Olive Hall
Milford, Ohio
February 1996

Zuza Said Goodbye

Every time I showed up to check on the house I was renting out, I saw Zuza on the other side of the fence. She belonged to Emilio and Genoveva Rodriguez who lived next door to the house I owned in Ponce, Puerto Rico. Zuza always barked at me and made a lot of noise. It was her way of declaring to the world that I was a stranger.

On December 31, 1977, I retired from my job. I decided to sell the house in which I was living and to settle in the house I had been renting. My move took place without a hitch and soon I was living next to Zuza's realm.

I have always liked animals. I am especially fond of dogs so I decided to do what I could to get on good terms with

Zuza. It wasn't easy. Zuza was of mixed collie and mongrel blood. She was intelligent like a collie and suspicious of people like a mongrel. Although her owners did not mistreat Zuza, they didn't spend much time petting her either. I thought she might be a little starved for affection.

At first the only thing I was able to do was to come near the fence, remain as still as possible, and observe her behavior. With each passing day she ventured a little closer to me until I let her sniff me through the fence.

The first time I touched her head with the tip of my fingers, it felt as if an electrical charge had passed through her. Every muscle in her body shook but she kept her ground, standing frozen on the spot and staring at me.

Before long we were good friends. When I passed by she would place her head near the fence to let me caress her. For about two years our friendship continued. Then on New Year's Day 1980 Zuza died of a heart attack.

Two days later something happened that I will never forget. I awoke at about 5:00 A.M. to see Zuza running in circles around my bed. The thought that she was dead did not enter my mind. She placed her front paws close to my face. I started to caress her head. After a while she resumed circling my bed—and the next moment she disappeared!

It was only then that I realized what had happened: Zuza had come back to say goodbye.

Vicente Albino
Ponce, Puerto Rico
August 1982

Frosty Came Back

I rescued my cat from a snow bank. It was a bitterly cold day when I looked out the kitchen window one morning and it was still snowing. As I looked, I heard a faint mewing sound. Just in front of the window I could see a small ball of dark fur.

I had quite a time getting the window open, because the ice held it fast, but I finally managed to open it a few inches, and there was a little cat face looking up at me. I reached out and I was able to pick the little animal up. I then wrapped towels around the cat and put it on a mat near the radiator. The poor little thing was shivering and shaking.

A little later I made some hot soup and fed it. The cat ate very slowly, looked his kitty thanks at me, and went to sleep. That evening he carefully explored the apartment.

Now that he was dry, I saw that he was a pretty cat, black and white except for russet patches on his forehead and chest. He was young, less than a year old. I asked around my neighborhood, but no one knew of a lost cat. So I adopted him and called him Frosty. When he recovered, he would cry loudly every evening to go out, but every morning he was there at the kitchen window asking to be let in.

Frosty stayed with me more than seven years. His favorite place to sleep was the rocking chair near my bed.

One morning, he was not at the window. When he did not appear for several days, I put "lost cat" posters up every place I could think of, because I really missed my kitty cat.

Late one night I could not sleep, so I put on my bed light and picked up the book on my night table. I had just read a few pages when I heard the rocking chair moving back and forth. I looked up, and there on the chair was Frosty, looking at me with a strange expression I had never seen before. I started to get up and go over to him, when, still looking at me, he gradually faded to a shadow.

I knew he must have met with an accident, but he came to say goodbye.

Adria Gillis
Long Beach, California
June 1996

My Friend, the Medium

The finest medium I've ever known was the late Albert M. DeForest of Buffalo, New York. By chance, in the third week of November 1966, shortly after my mother's death, I attended a Saturday night circle at the First Spiritual Temple in East Aurora where the Reverend DeForest was the minister.

When I, a total stranger, entered the séance room, he immediately remarked, "You think you came here alone but your mother rode with you in the front seat of your car. She's with you now." He then gave an accurate description of my mother, Ida Brader, and also a personal message.

Frequently thereafter I attended the Saturday night circles, and by summertime Al DeForest and his mother

Martha were my friends and had visited my home several times. Al always brought his cocker spaniel Duchess to frolic with my two dogs.

When Al succumbed after a cardiac attack on August 14, 1969, I was stunned and grief-stricken.

Exactly one year later I was working in my recreation room when my dogs' barking disturbed me. They came tumbling down the stairs and into the room followed by a dog I recognized as Al's Duchess and a strange collie-type dog. Since Duchess's death came shortly after her master's, I was astounded. Then Al himself materialized, romping with all four dogs.

"Al!" I exclaimed, forgetting he was a spirit. "With your heart condition you shouldn't be roughhousing."

He smiled, then said, "Marion, now I can do whatever I please." Then he and the visiting dogs vanished.

A few days later, when Mrs. DeForest showed me a snapshot of a dog named Tinker Belle whom Al once had owned, I recognized the "strange collie-type dog."

This experience has convinced me that life continues on another plane—for animals as well as people.

Marion Brader
West Seneca, New York
May 1974

Our "Dead" Cat

His name was Jada and my husband gave him to me for my birthday in April 1957. Tom had always claimed he did not like cats, so he chose a Siamese because he thought it would be more like a dog in temperament than other breeds of cat.

Jada lived with us for nine years before he died of a liver disease in July 1966. When we saw that Jada was not well we took him to the veterinarian for treatment. I spent my lunch hours rushing to visit him in his hospital cage and after several days was told to take him home because he might rally if surrounded by love.

He died in his favorite cool spot on the floor on a hot July day. I could not bear to disturb his body until the next morning when I buried him in a friend's garden near a beloved cat of her own.

I had to work that night at my job as reference librarian at Towson State University. I got through the time by not thinking of my dear Jada. When I arrived home about 10:30 that night, before I reached my door, Jada came running out to meet me as usual, curling around my feet.

As I bent to stroke him, I suddenly told myself, "But he's dead!" The cat disappeared.

My husband was in Florida at the time and it was not until a few days later that I wrote him of the cat's death. The day I mailed my letter to him was the day that I received one from him.

"I don't know what's going on around here," he wrote, "but last night I looked up and saw Jada lying near me on the couch. I felt a gentlemanly understanding pass between us. When I started to pet him he disappeared. Am I nuts or something?"

The letter was dated the day after Jada had died.

Louise H. S. Forshaw
Baltimore, Maryland
August 1982

Permanent Occupations
Spirits at Work

Many people identify very strongly with their occupations. Thus, it is not too surprising to find reports of ghosts on the job.

Here are a few stories concerning folks who were so attached to their vocations that even death could not tear them away.

The Boss from the Beyond

In the spring of 1955, I was working for an international trading firm run by three brothers. The oldest brother, Franklin, had leukemia. Though he grew weaker as his illness progressed, he continued to come to the office.

Franklin was a tall, gray-haired gentleman, heavyset, impeccably dressed and groomed, always courteous, and somewhat formal in his manner. The business was his life. He never took a vacation and his only trips had been business trips. When at last he was physically unable to come to work, the other brothers took him copies of the day's correspondence, which he kept under his pillow.

When Franklin died I went to his funeral. On the following Monday, the firm was open for regular business hours. I opened the office as usual at 8:30 A.M. The other offices on the floor were still dark at that hour, and it always seemed to me as if I worked in the only office in an empty building.

As I inserted my key into the door, I heard heavy footsteps inside. Jack, the middle brother, had spoken about having a safe installed, so I assumed that he had arranged to have the work done before the business day.

But as I opened the door, I was surprised to find that the office was still dark. I switched on the lights and saw that I was alone. At the teletype along the wall, the usual printout of cables extended to the floor. I acknowledged the messages, tore off the printout, and took it to my desk in the outer office. There I used the Boe Code book to decipher the messages. I liked this part of the day; it was like solving puzzles.

Just as I settled down, I heard a loud rustle of papers in the inner office where Franklin previously worked.

"The correspondence must be blowing all over the floor!" I thought. I hurried past the glass door and found the letters neatly piled on the desk under a paperweight. The window was closed.

I went back to my desk, my coffee, and the Boe Code. I had hardly sat down when the swivel chair creaked loudly and there was another rustling of paper. When I stood, I could see the inner office. The sounds ceased and nothing moved.

I sat down again. At once, the creak and the rustle sounded clearly. Again, I stood, and again all noises stopped. I sipped my coffee and read the cables. The creaking and rustling resumed.

"If Franklin wants to see the correspondence, let him," I decided and stayed at my desk. I knew he had no reason to harm me and I had none to disturb him, so we both went on with our work until nine o'clock, when the office day began and my colleague, Sylvia, arrived.

"I dreamed Franklin came back to the office," she said.

"He did," I told her. Sylvia and I talked it over and decided not to mention it to the surviving brothers, not knowing how they might react. We never told anyone about the episode, until now.

Charlotte A. Kellar
New York, New York
August 1997

The Night Joe Died

March 1928 was a month I'll never forget. A blizzard had been raging since shortly before dawn and when I took over the afternoon shift—9:30 A.M. to 1:00 P.M. at the Kensington station, 115th Street and Cottage Grove in Chicago, in the baggage room—the railroad tracks were covered with snow which piled higher as the hours passed. Trains were snowed in all down the line.

Kensington Station was a junction point, where trains for the south and east entered and left the Illinois Central right-of-way. Movement was controlled by tower-operated, interlocking switches, and these switches were giving the section gangs trouble. Clogging with snow, wet and packy, the whole line was tied up until they were cleared.

The snow stopped about sundown and the temperature dropped until at eight o'clock it registered five below zero. The drop in temperature added to our troubles. The switches froze solid and had to be thawed out with blow-torches. Smoke pots were then set up to keep them clear.

Number Nine, bound for Alabama and Florida, had a few passengers for both stops, and after flagging her down and getting the passengers and baggage aboard, I returned to the warmth of the baggage room. A quick look at the furnace showed that it was all right for a while so I dug out my lunch and set coffee going on the hot plate. There would be no other trains for two hours. I had time to eat and warm up.

I dozed in my chair with the station cat on my lap, and I guess I had slept for an hour or more when a voice woke me. I was startled to see the cat's back arched, and her tail fluffed out to three times its normal size. She was staring at one of our special agents, Joe Blainard, who had entered the luggage room.

He spoke urgently, "Sparky, there's a whole rail out under the Wildwood Crossover. Number Seventeen is due through there in about twenty minutes and you'd better notify the dispatcher."

With a hurried "Okay, Joe, and thanks!" I reached for the telephone. Before I had a chance to question him he turned and hurried out. I wondered about him as I went back to my chair.

The station closed at one in the morning and as I was locking the street door, the automatic telephone rang. It was the chief special agent.

"Sparky? How did you learn about that rail being out under the Wildwood Crossover?"

"Joe Blainard came to the baggage room and told me," I answered.

"What? Something's haywire somewhere . . . . You been drinking?"

"No sir! Why do you ask?" I replied.

"Sparky, Joe was killed at four o'clock at the Wildwood Crossover. We think he slipped while crossing the tracks. He was picked up at six o'clock, frozen stiff. He couldn't have talked to you at 11:40."

I could only insist that Joe had come to the baggage room. Finally, muttering that I must have been dreaming, the official hung up.

The story was later passed around as having been a dream and I let it go at that. But I was awake when Joe gave me his message.

Bob Farnham
Dalton, Georgia
December 1954

There Is No Death

No doubt many of you wonder, as you lay away the body of someone you love, what has become of the spirit, the life that made this loved one so wonderful.

I have the answer and I have had many experiences to prove this answer is right. I will tell you only one of these experiences.

After the First World War I moved to Milwaukee with my two small children. Milwaukee was a small town then, pleasant and easygoing. There I started a home bakery, employing two bakers, a candy maker, candy dipper, a dishwasher, delivery boy, and Bernice, a general helper.

I took Bernice from an orphanage when she just had completed her high-school course and was ready to support herself. She had been in the orphanage since she was six years old; both her parents were dead. The orphanage recommended her as honest, friendly, meticulous, and trustworthy. I found she was all these things and more.

Bernice sold bakery goods, opened the store in the mornings, and locked it at night. She kept the books, taking care of the receipts until Friday when she turned them over to me. I then paid the help and banked the balance on Saturday morning. As things were going, I wasn't going to get rich but I managed to support myself and two daughters.

About three years after Bernice started to work for me she met a nice young man and soon they became engaged. Since he was in dental school their marriage was not scheduled to take place for a time and I was glad I would have Bernice for a while longer.

One cold morning in March in the early 1900s I reached my bakery to find the door locked. I went around to the back wondering what had happened to Bernice. Then I opened the store and was so busy for the next few hours that thoughts of Bernice fled my mind.

About 10:00 A.M. there was a lull in the shop so I asked Dan, my delivery boy, to go to Tobar House where Bernice lived and learn why she was not at work. Dan started off on his bicycle. He returned soon bringing a police officer with him.

The officer started to question me, "You know Bernice Johnson?"

"Yes," I replied. "She works for me."

"Not any more," he said, "she's dead. Killed herself, it seems."

The man was gruff and unpleasant. "She have any family, friends, relatives?" he asked.

I was unable to answer many of the questions; practically all I knew was that Bernice had been raised in the orphanage and had no family. I told him she had a fiancé, but I didn't know his name except that she called him Tom and he attended a dental college. Which college, or where he roomed, I did not know.

Suddenly I remembered this was Friday and Bernice should have had the week's receipts from the bakery, which I needed to pay my employees. Of course, it was impossible to look in her room until the police ordered it unsealed, which could be days, weeks, or longer. My employees agreed to wait for their wages until I could make arrangements to pay them.

When the door was finally unsealed the room was searched thoroughly, but to no avail. I wondered if she had loaned the money to Tom in some emergency and then been ashamed to face me. Was this the reason for her suicide? Tom had disappeared from his rooming house and the police could not locate him. I became sure he had my money.

A few months later a friend dropped into my shop and asked if there were any clues as to why Bernice had taken her life. I told her my suspicions, that I was very unhappy about losing a week's receipts and didn't know how I would ever catch up. She asked if I ever had attended a Spiritualist meeting. I told her I had and was very much interested. She suggested we go to a meeting to be held that very night.

That evening a group of twelve of us sat down around a table at the home of the medium. The only illumination was from two candles; soft music from a phonograph filled the air. The medium impressed me as being an earthy type;

she was blonde and rather plump. But as it turned out she was very good.

The medium instructed us to hold hands and not let go since that would break the contact. We were to concentrate on the problem we wanted help with. After a few minutes she shivered as though with a sudden chill, then seemed to go into a trance. She called some of the guests by name and relayed messages to them from friends and relatives who had died.

Before long she turned to me, using my name and said, "There is a young girl standing next to you; she is crying so hard I can hardly understand what she is saying. Now I get it; she says, 'Tom should have married me now, but he is so stubborn. I couldn't live it down!'

"She is leaving; she crosses the room and goes down a flight of stairs, into a long narrow cellar apparently used as a storage room and crowded with barrels and boxes and tubs. She is walking to a corner. Here she stops and points toward the ceiling from which a heavy, dark brown string is dangling; now she has disappeared."

Was it possible this was the solution to my problem? I was so excited I could hardly wait for the meeting to end.

After we had said good night, my friend and I hurried to the bakery and down into the storeroom. In the corner, sure enough, there was the string. This we pulled and brought down the money bag I had been so sure I would never see again. All the money was there.

Now several mysteries were cleared up—why Bernice had taken her own life and that of her unborn child, and why Tom had disappeared.

Myra Stevens
Venice, California
April 1966

The Phantom Semi

My brother Danny Boatright died in December 1977 when the semi he was driving was involved in an accident near Mason, Texas. That same night my husband and I were driving from Carlsbad to San Antonio and I was asleep in the backseat when a nightmare awakened me. I remember saying, "There are no lights! I don't want to be dead!"

The words I spoke meant nothing to me until I learned that Danny had died that night. Then I felt bad because I thought I had had a message from him. He had not wanted to die.

Sometime during the first week of January my sisters Julia and Debra and I were playing with a tape recorder that had been a Christmas gift. We sat up very late that night and among the recordings we made was the song "Silver-haired Daddy" for our father W. W. Boatright. When we went to play it back, a strange thing happened. Instead of the song we heard what sounded like a CB transmission. Then we heard "West Texas Windmill" talking. That was Danny's CB handle.

We could not definitely identify his voice but we did get most of his message. He said, "Keep your trucks safe, brother truckers, and say your prayers," and "It's so beautiful—you wouldn't believe."

After midnight I took the recorder to my mother, who had been having trouble sleeping since Danny's death. I knew she would want to hear the message. She planned to send the tape to a psychic for explanation, but the tape was lost in a fire before she could do so.

Whenever Danny left on a run he would tell Mother he would be back—meaning, of course, in the flesh. But he has come back many times since his death. On his birthday we have heard a semi pull up to the house, and we have even seen its lights! Then we hear the air brakes and the door opening and slamming shut. When we go outside, there is no truck to be seen anywhere.

Whenever this happens, Mother says Danny is just letting her know he has come back.

Rebecca Boatright Chapman
Water Valley, Texas
April 1984

Restless Spirits

Ghost Stories!

Some spirits seem to be attached to a location important to them in their earthly lives. Interaction with such lingering presences can be compelling evidence that "the spirit lives on."

While many of our stories so far have concerned brief, benign visits from deceased family members or friends, the reports in this chapter feature mysterious earthbound spirits—some simply lonesome, some indifferent, and some decidedly unfriendly. Here we present a selection of *FATE*'s most intriguing ghost stories.

Haunted in California

Following my mother's death in 1992, my husband, sons, and I had two choices. We could continue to rent the house we were living in, or move into my mother's old house and renovate. We asked the boys for their opinion, and they agreed with us that it would be fun to take the old place and make it ours.

Perhaps it was because we were so busy that we noticed nothing out of the ordinary at first. I do know that the first incident was one that I brushed aside—quite literally!

I was with my mother when she had her fatal heart attack in the bathroom that we were remodeling, and in which the first strange occurrence took place. I had always dreamed of having a carpeted bathroom, so my husband had a beautiful carpet installed after the room was painted, and an antique mirror was hung over the basin. Very soon after these changes, I got up one night to use the bathroom, only to discover that the carpet had been brushed backward, as if with a fingernail, to spell the words: "Go Away!"

Shades of Amityville! Did I feel chills, get goosebumps, and scream? No—like any intelligent mother, I suspected a prank. I brushed the carpet back and thought no more of it.

We continued to remodel the house, and I began to delve into my mother's past in search of answers for questions that were bothering me. Every fact I uncovered exposed lies she had told about herself, and raised more questions.

My husband began to complain of feeling cold when he was downstairs, and of noticing a shadowy figure out of the corner of his eye while he was alone in the house. My youngest son declared that he was awakened late one night by the sound of footsteps coming up the stairs, accompanied by the rattle of a cup and saucer. He had no way of knowing that it was my mother's habit to stay up late watching television, and to bring her empty demitasse cup and saucer (which rattled because she had hand tremors) upstairs when she retired.

One very still afternoon, when I was alone in the house, I heard the first few tinkling notes of a music box tune, and all was quiet again. The problem: My mother's music box collection had been put in storage.

These events were so infrequent that we did not pay them much attention. However, something happened during the holiday season that made it impossible to deny that something very strange and inexplicable was going on in our home. My mother had always made sweet potato pie for the boys. Following her death, I had discontinued the practice, but the boys' nagging finally got me to make one for Thanksgiving dinner in 1994. A sweet potato pie is the last thing you slide into the oven, so I called to my husband and told him to put the cats and dogs outside while I set the table. When it was done, I called the boys in to taste it. They promptly (and loudly) pronounced it better than my mother's.

As this was going on, we heard a crash from the bathroom, and I yelled at my husband, "Why did you put the cats in the bathroom?" I assumed that the commotion was somehow pet-related. We rushed into the bathroom to survey the damage. The antique mirror that we had hung over the basin now rested, unbroken, on the floor—as if someone had yanked it from the wall and tossed it across the room in a fit of anger!

Later, a close friend of mine heard the unmistakable sound of my mother's breathing (she was a two-pack-a-day smoker), and then saw the carpet indent, as if from footprints. This same friend had her hair pulled by an unseen hand while sitting in our dining room.

One overnight guest heard heavy breathing coming up the stairs; another heard footsteps in the kitchen. Our dogs often awaken from sleep and howl for no apparent reason. The television shuts itself off, switches to sports (my mother's favorite pastime), or switches to the channel that we have locked, whose message reads (prophetically?): "This channel is parentally controlled."

Elizabeth Phillips-Miravalle
Clearlake Oaks, California
February 2000

Spectral Lovers

About the year 1948, when my husband Frank and I were just dating, we had the most unusual experience either of us has ever had. One Saturday night that August, Frank and I double-dated with our friends Fred and Debbie. We turned on to a side road off Whitney Avenue in Hamden, Connecticut, and stopped the car near a bridge to catch a breath of air.

When Frank turned off the car lights, all four of us saw two white figures ahead. They appeared to be a man and woman in wedding attire, standing about ten feet in front of our car. Frank quickly switched the headlights back on but the two figures had vanished. Thinking we must have imagined them, Frank turned the lights off again, where-upon the two pale figures reappeared.

We started the car and headed for home, all four of us feeling as pale as the two ghostly lovers had looked.

We were all familiar with a certain local legend concern-ing a young couple who wanted to get married but were forbidden to do so by their parents. The desperate young lovers ran off one night and committed suicide by jumping from that very bridge. This had happened many years ago before we were born—or so the story went.

Frank and I never went back to that spot at night. I often wonder if anyone else ever saw the young couple.

I still get a chill every time I recall these tragic young lovers in their wedding attire.

Lyda Zentek (as told to Carol Ann Zentek)
Cheshire, Connecticut
August 1976

Ghost Who Tooled Around

In 1993, after living in apartments for most of our married life, my husband and I purchased a home. The house was about seventy years old, and had been refurbished by the owner, a young man. I felt peace emanating from within the very first time that I entered the home.

After moving in and getting settled, I talked to a neighbor who had owned the home prior to the young man. The neighbor told me that a couple (since deceased) had owned it. I then asked if they had been religious, and the neighbor informed me that there had been a grotto of the Virgin Mary in their backyard. However, when the young man had purchased the home, he removed the grotto.

Two months later, my husband and I were awakened one evening by footsteps on the stairs. We heard those noises many more times.

I decided to research the history of the deceased couple via home ownership papers. I discovered that the woman's first name was the same as my middle name, and that she had worked with abused children. I was savagely abused when I was a child. From the neighbor, I learned that the old man liked to work with tools.

One morning, I took a laundry basket full of clothes into the basement and was shocked to see a bunch of tools strewn around the cement floor. I jokingly asked my husband if he had had a wild night flinging tools around the basement. He scratched his head, and asked why. When I told him that the old man had been at it again, my husband knew exactly who I meant.

Topping this off, we also found a large bolt right in the middle of our living room floor one morning. We nearly stumbled over it, and had never seen it before.

At five o' clock every morning, our home would become like a refrigeration unit as my husband and I shivered. We wondered if our heating system was on the blink, so we had it checked but nothing was wrong with it. I began to become more inquisitive about the old man who had owned our home so long ago.

I asked our neighbor if anybody had died in our home, and at what time—specifically, whether it had happened in the dining room, since that is where I did some of my best writing and photography. (I had even written a poem titled "Whispers in My Dining Room" prior to speaking with my neighbor.) When my neighbor finally relented and told me that the old man had indeed died in our dining room, I wasn't the least bit surprised since I had already surmised it.

My husband and I have since relocated, but we miss that old home. We truly loved it.

M. Cathy Helms
Webster, New York
October 2000

Haunted Harold House

In March 1996, I traveled from my home in Louisiana to Portland, Oregon, to attend a grooming school for four months. There were students from all over the country who attended this school. The owner of the school also owned two houses within a block of each other that were used for student housing. I lived at the "Harold House"—so named because it was located on Harold Avenue. At the time, there were four of us renting this particular house.

I sensed that there was a presence within the house from the moment I arrived. The basement was unoccupied, and the door leading to it was beside the staircase leading to my bedroom, which I shared with a girl from Singapore. Almost on a daily basis, my housemates and I would find the basement door open when none of us had opened it. We thought that possibly a draft of some sort had pushed it open while we were at school, so we would close it and not think anything about it.

One day at school, my roommate was acting unusually standoffish toward me. At lunchtime, when everyone else was outside, I asked her what was the matter.

She glared at me angrily and said, "What's the matter! You want to know what's the matter? I'll tell you what's the matter. You kept me awake half the night talking in your sleep!"

I apologized and asked her what I was saying. She said I was talking like I was meeting someone for the first time— asking their name, how old were they, where were they from, and so on.

I told her that she should have awakened me and told me to be quiet. She stated that she was going to, but when she turned over in her bed to wake me up, she saw a large white bath towel floating between our beds, so she just closed her eyes and rolled back over facing the wall.

After my roommate made this statement, our instructor (who was also present in the room, although we were not aware that she was listening to our conversation) exclaimed, "*Oh my God!*"

She was staring at us wide-eyed with her hands over her mouth.

Now my curiosity was aroused. I asked our instructor what was wrong. She then explained to us that a couple of years prior, a male student who lived in the basement of our house had died of a drug overdose. His body was found the next afternoon with a white bath towel wrapped around his waist. We learned that his name was Mark. She further explained that the owners of the school did not want the instructors telling students about this incident. We promised her that we wouldn't tell anyone.

At our house, the basement door continued to open by itself every day. One afternoon, all my housemates were downstairs at the kitchen table talking. I decided to go downstairs and join the group. As I exited my bedroom, I caught a glimpse of someone standing against the wall between my room and the bathroom. At first I dismissed it, thinking it was one of my male housemates, but I thought it was odd that he would just be standing there. I stopped in my tracks and turned to look.

The person standing there was not one of my male housemates. Although I could see the outline of his body, it was transparent. I could see that his hair and mustache were dark colored. I realized that I was possibly seeing Mark's ghost. We stood there in the hall, staring at each other for several seconds before he suddenly faded away.

The next day at school, I went to my instructor and asked her what Mark looked like. She said he was good looking, a little taller than me, and had dark hair and a mustache. I smiled and told her that I thought I saw him the night before, standing by my bedroom in the hall. When I described him, she was amazed. Although former students who lived in the house had always complained of the basement door opening by itself, I was the only one who had ever seen him. She wondered why he would choose to show himself to me. I guess I'll never know.

Lisa Perry
Houston, Texas
July 2000

The Punch

The security alarm rang at 2:00 A.M. in the empty house. When we were notified, we rushed to the rambling ranch house that we had just purchased. There was no sign of forced entry. Examining the interior, we discovered that the pantry door had swung wide open and set off the alarm.

This happened in 1989. It was the first of many instances of doors opening and closing by themselves. We attributed this to faulty hinges and drafts. Then the toilets began to flush by themselves.

The house had been vacant for three years. It needed redecorating and repairs before we could move in. For three months I directed painters, plumbers, and carpenters.

One afternoon after the workmen departed, I was standing in the kitchen when I heard one of the toilets flush. This irritated me. I had spent eight hundred dollars to fix the toilets and none had malfunctioned for weeks. Then the door to the kitchen moved. I couldn't see anything or anyone, but I felt a presence.

"Look," I told it. "I'm the new owner. I bought and paid for this house, and I want you out. Get out! Now!"

Suddenly, I felt a sharp blow to the chest. I doubled over in pain. My first thought was that I had worked myself into a such a snit that I was having a heart attack. Then I opened my blouse. At the point of pain, there was a red mark the size of a fist. This was not my imagination. I could see the bruise as well as feel it.

Feeling somewhat foolish, I spoke to the presence. "Okay. You made your point. If you insist on hanging around, please stay out of my way."

So began my relationship with the ghost of the former occupant of my home. For months the toilet would flush properly, but then it would suddenly flush at night when I stepped into the bathroom. Objects would tumble from my dressing table when I hadn't touched them. Several times when I typed the name of the previous owner on my computer, the screen suddenly went blank.

In one way, the ghost seemed helpful. The previous occupant had been a multimillionaire with great financial savvy. My own investments were quite profitable during this time— evidence, perhaps, of direction from beyond?

Caroline Totten
Canton, Ohio
February 1999

Lucinda, Child of Long Ago

Many years ago, when I was a small child, I met a young girl about my own age. Her name was Lucinda. She rarely spoke, but we spent many hours playing together one particular summer. She would only come to play if I was alone. She was always dressed the same: a white dress with ruffles, white stockings, and black shoes. She always carried a beautiful doll with her. The resemblance between Lucinda and the doll was uncanny. The only difference seemed to be that Lucinda had long, dark hair in rag curls and the doll had blonde hair in rag curls.

I asked Lucinda where she lived, but she never responded to the question. One day, toward the end of summer, Lucinda walked out of my backyard and I decided to follow her. Down the alley from my house there was an old, two-story house. I noticed Lucinda go through the open back gate to this house's yard and disappear in its lush garden.

When I reached the open gate, I looked inside, searching for Lucinda. She had vanished! Yet there had not been enough time for her to leave the garden. I was very confused by this.

School would start the following week and I had not seen Lucinda for several days. I decided to go to the house where I thought she lived. I walked around the block to the front of the house, opened the small gate, walked up to the front door, and rang the bell. A few moments later, a lady opened the door. I asked her if her little girl could come out and play.

The lady replied, "We don't have a little girl," and slammed the door in my face.

I never saw Lucinda again. Many times I would walk down the alley and peek through her fence, hoping to see her in her garden. I never did.

Years later, as an adult, I was at the cemetery placing flowers on the graves of friends and family. As I walked through the grounds, I glanced at the old headstones that displayed pictures of the deceased. I stopped and stared as one of these headstones came into view. On it was an oval picture of Lucinda. She was wearing the pretty white dress that I remembered.

I looked at the date on the headstone. Lucinda was born in 1883 and died in 1891. Her life had been cut short years before I was born. Perhaps her visits with me were a way for her to enjoy a bit of the childhood she had never really had.

I had one rose left and I gently placed it on her grave, remembering this small child that I had played with many years ago.

Elizabeth Smith
Tulare, California
November 1996

Vision in the Cottage

In 1946 I bought a little cottage on the slope between Mount Tamalpais and the Pacific Ocean, with a broad view of open pastures and woods. Across the bay at night I can see the glittering lights of San Francisco.

I was very weary the day I moved in and retired early, my mind busy with things that had to be done, particularly with the problem of a leaky roof. While musing on how to proceed I looked down the dark hall and, although I knew I was alone in the house, I saw a woman standing there. She seemed to belong to the house, and I was not at all startled. There was a smile on her sweet face when she saw that she had my attention. Coming closer she said "My dear, have you said your prayers? Do not forget them."

The following day I described the woman to several neighbors. They said immediately, "Why, that is Mrs. P., who lived there."

It seems that Mrs. P. and her husband built the house as a haven in which to spend their last days, but they died before they could realize their dreams.

Mrs. P. was very religious, playing the organ and singing in church, but I had not known this previously.

As long as I live in this little cottage I shall thank God for leading me here and for leaving such a kindly spirit to guard me.

In other houses where I have lived I have felt vibrations of previous tenants and have come to believe that when a person touches something they leave an indelible mark.

Jessie Kenyon
Bolinas, California
July 1955

The Covers-Up Ghosts

One morning at the breakfast table, I made a simple statement to William, my husband: "Honey, I think there are ghosts in our home."

William didn't even flinch. Finishing a sip of coffee, he calmly looked at me and said, "I think so too. I didn't want to say anything to you because I thought you would get scared. What makes you think we have ghosts?"

I told William that when I woke up that morning, I had sensed a group of spiritual entities rushing out of our bedroom. It was like I had interrupted something they were doing. I didn't catch a glimpse of them, but I did see the bedroom's double doors moving slightly as they left.

William didn't question my story. He had also had a weird experience during the night. He said something had covered up his feet with the small afghans we keep at the foot of our bed. Something had also pulled the covers up over his back. At first he thought it was me, but then he saw that I was sound asleep.

"I've also seen shadows floating across the bedroom, and once I felt a breeze as if someone had just moved past me," William continued, nonplussed.

A few weeks later, I was taking an afternoon nap when I was interrupted by a hard slap on my feet. Startled, I looked up and saw circular discs floating across the ceiling. I watched until they disappeared.

Another time, walking out of our closet, I saw a cloudy white form standing across the room. I felt a chill. When I yelled for William, the form disappeared.

I did research to see if anyone had died in the house. There had been an alcoholic, a person admitted to a rest home, and a woman who was partially blind and had painted the tips of the light switches red so she could see them, but no one had died there.

After much discussion William and I decided to ask our minister to bless our home. We didn't tell her what we had found out about the house. When the minister came, we sat in the living room and meditated. I felt a sense of peace.

"I sense there was an alcoholic here," the minister said as she opened her eyes. She rubbed sage on places where she felt a cold spot. She said this was an old Cherokee custom taught to her by her mother, who was part Cherokee.

Our minister went through each room in the house, telling us what she felt. She found cold spots in our bathroom, the walk-in closet, and the corner in the sunroom, where the partially blind lady used to do her handiwork. Then we told the minister the history of the house.

"I want you to burn vanilla candles for two to four hours in these cold places," she told us. "Do this every afternoon. Spirits do not like the smell of vanilla."

Two nights after we first burned the candles, I woke suddenly, and my attention was drawn to the sliding glass door leading into the sunroom. I saw five shadowy figures standing in the drapes. They were dressed according to different time periods and were both male and female. This lasted for several seconds, which seemed like an eternity. I couldn't speak. I wanted to get up but was too afraid. Finally, they disappeared. Maybe they were saying farewell.

Things were quiet after that until my ten-year-old grandson, Cass, came to visit. The first morning Cass was with us, he asked me, "What are we going to do after lunch, Nana?"

"Rest, read, visit, or nap," I replied.

"Well, Nana, we could talk about ghosts," he said. "Your house is haunted. Did you know that?"

I was astonished. We hadn't told him about the ghosts. "What makes you think so?" I stammered.

"Well, last night, I heard a voice coming from the guest closet. It was laughing and it woke me up."

"Oh, really, Cass, you must have been dreaming."

"Nana, you don't believe me, do you? I saw the reflection of a man's head and shoulder in the mirror in the corner of your bedroom." This is the corner where I had seen the white form. "That's not all," he continued. "The man was wearing a hat with a feather in it and he had black, curly hair. And I have seen shadows dashing back and forth."

I told him the whole story about our experiences with ghosts. He was excited.

Since we moved, we kind of miss the excitement of having the ghosts. Whenever we left for a vacation, we told them goodbye and to have a good time while we were gone. It seemed like the right thing to do.

Edythe Ve Del Spitler
La Habra, California
May 1999

Catholic School Rebels

In the early 1970s I enrolled as a freshman in a small Catholic women's college. Upon arriving, I was directed to Mara Hall, the oldest dormitory on campus. The stained-glass windows and long, dark hallways made me feel like I had walked onto a Gothic movie set. My room at the end of the building was very large and bright. But it was so quiet that I started having second thoughts about coming early.

My four roommates and I all hit it off instantly, except for one from the Philippines. She had strange ideas about our room, and before the day was over, she insisted on transferring to another room, saying ours "felt wrong."

The rest of us were a rowdy bunch. We blasted heavy metal music all the time and transformed our room into "blacklight heaven." We took the mattresses off the bed frames and put them on the floor. This wasn't dormitory policy, but we didn't exactly follow the rules.

The first week went by without incident, but then small things started happening. Personal items would disappear and then reappear a few days later where they were last seen. The volume on the stereo would adjust by itself. We started locking our door. We even reported these events to our dorm mother.

One afternoon I decided to skip lunch and go back to our room to study. After a period of time I had the strangest feeling I was being watched. I looked up from my book to find a short, elderly nun standing next to my bed.

I was shocked to see her, and even more so when she called me by name and began lecturing me on the appearance of the room. I was eighteen years old, and wasn't in the mood for a lecture. I assured her that we would straighten it up and went back to my book. Then it hit me—I had locked the door.

In that amount of time the nun had disappeared.

Sandy Baughman
Irwin, Pennsylvania
October 1999

Amanda

The soft, misty figure of a woman stood on our back porch. My husband Gerald caught sight of her out of the corner of his eye and he was within a few feet of her when she vaporized. This was our introduction to the resident spirit in our new home.

Within our first year here (1980), after the spirit made her presence known, we requested an abstract on our home and property. The land grant was given in 1842, and Joseph and Matilda Bailie received title to the land upon completion of the log house. We learned a residence had to be constructed within a year for people to keep title to the land, according to the law in those days. The homestead was sold in 1876 when new additions were built.

Over the next few years our ghost, whom we affectionately named Amanda (not Matilda), became part of our family. What Gerald saw was not very definite, but from time to time we heard her clearly. On one occasion we were in our bedroom talking and carrying on. From the corner of the room we heard a voice say in a severe tone, "Stop it! I said, stop it!" Boy, did we!

Another time I was alone in the house. It was spring and all the windows were open. I heard laughter from outside and thinking it was a neighbor and her kids walking up, I went outside. There was no one there. Coming back in and resuming my work, I heard the laughter one more time. I chuckled and said, "Okay, Amanda, the joke's up." And that was the end of it.

Sometime later my husband was getting ready to go to work on the midnight shift. As he kissed me goodbye, he casually mentioned that Amanda was at the top of the stairs. I was thrilled.

We have been restoring the house and Amanda took a keen interest in every step. We concluded that Amanda (Matilda) was the first owner of the house because she appeared only in that original part of the building.

When Gerald and I decided to put the kitchen back where it was originally, hearth and all, Amanda stopped appearing. It seems so empty here now. Did Amanda want only to know her house was being cared for? Of course I'm glad if she's happy, but we do miss her.

Susan M. Anton
Cedar Hill, Missouri
December 1987

Candy's Mansion

Have you ever lived in a haunted house? I have. In 1953 my family—my parents Mary and Haywood Moore, my brothers Gary and John, and I—moved into a large green house on Peck Hill Road in Perrysburg, New York. Neighbors referred to it as "Candy's mansion" from the name of a previous owner and warned us that it was haunted. We moved in anyway.

From the very first we heard unexplained noises. Many times, day or night, while sitting in the living room we would hear footsteps and dishes rattling upstairs. For most of the year we kept the upstairs empty and sealed off because it was difficult and expensive to heat. There never were any people (or dishes!) up there at the times we heard the noises. Sometimes we went up to the vacant floor to investigate but never found any explanation for the sounds. Indeed we could hear the noises around us, even in the same room with us, but never saw anyone to cause them.

The most frightening incident occurred in late January 1954. One night we heard an unusual assortment of loud noises—footsteps, dishes rattling, and other indescribable sounds. It even sounded as if dishes were being broken.

Finally my father declared someone had to be up there. He unlocked and opened the door leading upstairs and we all felt an oppressive chill unlike anything we had felt before. Dad ordered our collie up to investigate—he normally was a fine watchdog—but after going only halfway up the stairs he turned around with his tail between his legs and ran back down to hide.

Dad announced that if whatever was up there scared the dog that badly, it could wait until daylight. We all went to bed but I don't think any of us slept much that night. The noises continued until dawn.

The next day we checked all the outside entrances but found no signs of entry. Then Dad drove to town and returned with a few friends and the local constable. We all went upstairs to investigate. In one of the empty, dust-covered bedrooms we saw a sight I shall never forget.

Bare footprints began in the middle of the large room and headed toward the wall, finally leaving only a heel print showing on our side of the wall. In the next room we found that the footprints continued into the middle of that room and there stopped as abruptly as they had begun in the other room. The prints began and ended at least eight feet from the nearest door of either room and about six feet from the nearest window. We saw no way anyone could have gotten into the rooms to make the tracks, let alone how he could have walked through a solid wall.

One of the men from town left immediately after seeing the tracks and never came to our house again. The others tried to figure out a logical explanation but gave up in despair and finally left. After this none of them cared to return to the house. We moved out in August 1955, and as far as I know the ghost lives there yet.

Daniel A. Moore
White Sands, New Mexico
June 1974

Ghosts in Residence

In the fall of 1955, when my twin sister and I were seven years old, our family moved to Harvard, Illinois, into a house that turned out to be haunted. It was a typical turn-of-the-century house with a kitchen, dining room, living room, and den on the first floor, three bedrooms and a bath on the second floor, and a front porch. The house was situated on a corner lot.

When my family moved in it was evident there had never been much remodeling done. Only the kitchen and bathroom had been modernized. The house was basically the same as it had been when it was built.

My father did quite a bit of work on the house over several years, along with beautifying the yard and painting the outside of the house. He also wallpapered inside, letting me choose the wallpaper for the bedroom that my sister and I shared. He also painted the garage at the back of the yard. We were proud of the property's finished look as compared to the original rather dingy appearance it had when we moved in.

I mention all of this because I believe that the ghost I am going to tell you about also approved of these changes.

The first few years we lived in this house my sister and I, along with our younger sister who was five years old at the time and had her own bedroom, all saw a smiling lady standing by our beds. We always saw her at night—not every night, just now and then. She seemed to glow in her own "light" and wore a long dress of a floral patterned material. Her hair seemed to be put up on her head in a bun. She didn't frighten us; as a matter of fact, she exuded a rather happy feeling. It was as if she was just checking on us to make sure all was well.

We spoke of this to our mother, who didn't believe us. By the time we had lived there three or four years we stopped seeing the ghost but I do believe she was still there.

Another occurrence we experienced periodically while we lived in that house always happened late at night. Because Father was a sound sleeper he never heard a thing, but the rest of us all did. We would be awakened about one or two in the morning by loud voices talking and laughing, although we could not make out anything they were saying. There would also be the sound of glasses tinkling. It sounded as if some kind of party were in progress.

The first time we heard this my sister and I thought we had company. We got out of bed and went to the top of the stairs. We peered down into the dining room but it was pitch-black. Nevertheless the noises continued all around us and there was a "coldness" that seemed to permeate the whole house. I looked at my sister and she looked at me and without a word we scooted back to the safety of our bed and pulled the covers over our heads.

Our younger sister and Mother were awakened periodically by this same party. Neither of them ever got up to investigate and my twin sister and I never got up again. What the source of this was I don't know, but the atmosphere in the house was not normal when this occurred.

The night my sister and I got up to check on the noises it was in the middle of winter and the house was shut up tightly. Our neighbors all went to bed fairly early and were not party givers. And none of their homes were close to our house anyway.

I remember the eerie feeling we got when these parties were held. It was not a "happy" feeling as it was when the lady-ghost was around. It seems the house had at least two different spirits haunting it.

In the spring of 1961 the house was sold and we made plans to move to another city when school was out. By this time I was twelve years old. One day I happened to be the only one home and I was standing in the living room looking out the window. I was thinking how much I liked the house and how sorry I was we had to leave it.

All of a sudden I heard something drop onto the rug right behind me. I turned around and there, lying on the floor, was a gold bar pin—the kind of dress pin women used to wear back in the "old days." I picked it up and looked up at the ceiling but there was nothing to see. I even got a chair to stand on and looked more closely at the ceiling. There just weren't any holes there.

When my mother returned I showed it to her and suggested that perhaps the lady ghost had materialized it so I would have a memento of "our" house after we left.

I still have this bar pin; it's not every day a ghost makes a tangible gift to a living person!

Margaret M. Downing
Machesney Park, Illinois
May 1987

The Mayor

In 1968 my family and I lived in a four-story house in Hamden, Connecticut. Every night I woke up at two o'clock and saw a man dressed in a black cape and tall hat. I either saw his shadow on the hallway walls or saw him breeze by me. I moved into another bedroom, but these things still happened.

One night as I was sleeping, I felt a presence in my room and hot air blowing on my back. Crying hysterically, I ran downstairs to tell my mother, Rosemarie Ferraro. I told her everything. Because I was young, she didn't make an issue out of it. She told me that I was just having nightmares.

When I grew older and Mom realized that I had ESP, she confessed that my story had amazed her. The man whom I had seen (Michael J. Whalen) had lived in the house years ago. He died there and I was seeing his ghost. I saw him dressed in a hat and cape because he was a former mayor of the town. When she bought the house my mom had seen a picture of him wearing those clothes. I believe that he knew I was psychic.

After this I took my psychic abilities very seriously, and so did everyone else.

Ann Marie Longobardi
New Haven, Connecticut
November 1994

My Experience with a Ghost

During the 1970s I ran our family business in a nineteenth-century building in the courthouse square of Georgetown, Texas. When Grandmother was taken to a nursing home, her belongings were moved to the store's second floor. A few pieces of furniture, including her favorite rocking chair, went to my house.

Shortly after Grandmother passed away, I noticed some picture albums and a crocheted bedspread in an unsealed box. I left them because my hands were full.

Several days later, Amy, a clerk at the store, was taking some things upstairs, so I asked her to bring the box down. She returned pale and upset and told me that when she had started to pick up the box, she had felt someone watching her. She turned and saw a small, gray-haired lady sitting in a rocking chair in the corner. Amy knew she was alone upstairs and that there was no rocking chair in the room. She left the box and came downstairs quickly.

The next day I brought the box downstairs. Amy and the other clerks crowded around as I began to go through the pictures.

Suddenly Amy exclaimed, "That's her!" pointing to a woman in a group photo.

"Who?" I asked.

Amy said she was the lady in the rocking chair. The woman in the photo was my grandmother. I suppose she was looking after her belongings. She never liked strangers touching her things.

Shortly after that, everything was moved to my house, and my grandmother has not been seen again.

Jane R. Montgomery
Georgetown, Texas
May 1996

Ghost to the Rescue

My mother's dear friend Phyllis Jenkins lived in Mount Martha, Victoria, Australia, not far from my parents' house. Phyllis had been widowed for many years and Mother used to visit her weekly for a friendly Bible reading. Over the years they had grown very close, and it was shortly after they met that Phyllis told Mum her true ghost story.

When Phyllis had been a young newlywed, shortly after World War II, she had stayed in a friend's house in Queensland with her husband and their small son. After a stay of a few months the friends moved out, but Phyllis and her family stayed on for several years as tenants. The house was a typical Queensland home, a weatherboard on stilts. But there was something atypical about its atmosphere.

Apparently, one night as Phyllis was in the bathroom, she was startled when a large man walked past the open doorway. Other than her sleeping son, she was the only occupant in the house at the time. Phyllis searched all the rooms, but she could find no trace of the man.

When her husband and friends returned later that evening, she told them about her encounter.

"So you've met our captain," her girlfriend said.

She then went on to explain that apparently the house was haunted by the ghost of a sea captain. He was not seen very often, and then only passing the bathroom when the door was open.

Phyllis didn't know whether to join in the laughter about her encounter or to be frightened about the ghost. After some time had passed, however, having not seen the ghost again, she put the episode out of her mind.

A few months later, Phyllis took her son to the beach for a swim. The tide was a long way out, and they merrily splashed their way from one sandbank to another until they were quite a distance from shore. Suddenly, the sand beneath their feet gave way and they began to sink. Somehow they had found a small stretch of quicksand, and before they could move, their ankles were firmly grasped by the slippery substance, which was pulling them down further. Panicking, Phyllis tried to pull her son out of the quicksand, but her struggles only sank them deeper.

Suddenly, from nowhere, two strong arms ripped them from the sand sucking around their calves and carried them away from danger. Shocked by the horror of the quicksand, Phyllis barely registered that the strong arms belonged to the sea captain.

After a short distance, Phyllis and her son were abruptly set on their feet, standing on a firm sandbank closer to shore. Phyllis turned around to thank their savior, but found no one. Turning wildly from side to side, she could not see anyone—they were surrounded by open sand and water. Nobody could have disappeared so quickly.

Puzzled but grateful, Phyllis sent a swift prayer of thanks to heaven and quickly made her way back to the beach.

From that time until they moved to Victoria, Phyllis and her family saw the ghost of the sea captain on a number of occasions, always passing the bathroom door. She always said "Thank you" when he passed, although he never acknowledged her. The house took on a feeling of security, one that she missed greatly when she finally moved away.

Karin Dallas
Mornington, Victoria, Australia
June 1996

Someone Lives with Us

We rented the top half of a duplex apartment on April 17, 1974, but didn't know until a year later that it was haunted. Or perhaps it wasn't haunted, and we brought the ghost into it along with an antique clock or some other old piece we cherish.

My husband Bob and I were lying in bed talking when we both caught sight of a strange gray shadow moving in the kitchen. It was a misty shape but seemed to be an old man wearing a hat and coat. It glided from our boy's room, through the kitchen, and into the bathroom. We ceased our conversation as we watched the apparition in amazement.

I thought I was seeing things and asked Bob if he saw anything walking around in the kitchen. After further discussion we agreed we had seen the ghost of an old man.

In the months that followed strange things began to happen. Our year-old son, who previously had cried a lot, began to giggle at night in his dark bedroom and to talk, in his own way, to "someone" I couldn't see.

One time I was drawing a bath when a pencil fell straight out of the air. It hit my head and landed in the water. Another time I was bent over the wastebasket peeling potatoes when out of the corner of my eye I saw a heavy statue "fall" off the top of the refrigerator, miss my head by an inch, and land in the trash behind me.

Things belonging to my husband and me would disappear and reappear again mischievously. We decided the "old man" liked to hide things from us.

One evening when my husband and I were about to make love, a screw fell from the air and landed right beside my husband. There was no place on the ceiling it could have come from. Obviously, our ghost has a sense of humor.

One February morning in 1975 Bob and I heard heavy footsteps coming up our stairs and then a knock on our front door. Bob answered the door but no one was there. There were footprints in snow leading up the stairs but none going back down. We had to attribute this visit to our phantom.

By September that same year I began to think seriously of having a priest bless our home but my husband was opposed to this. So I resorted to shouting, "Ghost, I don't want to hate you but if you don't behave I will. We both can live in this house peacefully!"

A few days later I was putting on my army jacket when I found my favorite gold earrings in the left breast pocket. I had lost them somewhere outside weeks before. I asked Bob about the earrings but he had no idea how they had ended up in the jacket, which no one had worn for months.

That same day I had to use this jacket to put out a fire I had started by accident in the garage. I had put a dollar bill in the left breast pocket but had forgotten about it until Bob mentioned it. The jacket was ruined, burned to a few black rags, and the left pocket almost completely burned away. But when I shook the charred rags, the dollar bill—still green with just a small edge of black—fell out. The old man must have heard me when I shouted at him.

He has a bad habit of opening locked doors at night and leaving them wide open, or knocking at the door in the morning. He proves it is he by leaving no footsteps in the snow. But he has proven—just as I told him—we can live together peacefully so long as we put up with each other's peculiarities.

Mary Booth
Salem, Ohio
September 1976

Curtain Calls
Supernatural Communication
at the Moment of Death

Many of the stories of survival collected by *FATE* concern paranormal visits from distant loved ones that take place at the very instant of passing.

What unique circumstance allows for such things to happen—a special dispensation by the powers that be allowing a final farewell? A surge of spiritual energy as the soul is released from the physical realm? We can only imagine; perhaps someday we will know.

The Glow in the Corner

The day before my cousin Jon Burns's birthday party, I was in the back seat of the family car, going to stay overnight at the house of my friends, Patti and Chris Thelen, who lived near Jon. In the morning my parents, Sam and Edith Rose, were to pick me up on their way to Jon's party. My mind wandered to my grandfather, Eli Rose, whom I hadn't seen in a long time.

Grampa Rose and I were pals, and very close. He was seventy-eight and I was twelve, but we understood each other. He believed in me and supported my goals. A twelve-year-old girl gets some wild ideas, but Grampa backed me up. He called me "Susie Poosie," which was evidence of our feelings about each other, for I would only tolerate such a silly nickname from someone I loved dearly.

Grampa Rose was a tall, dignified man who wore wire-rimmed glasses and was almost totally bald. He always sported dark wool pants and a long-sleeved white shirt, no matter what the season or weather. Occasionally he'd don a brown argyle mohair sweater, but he still wore the shirt underneath.

He smoked expensive cigars, read classic books, and listened to classical music, decorating his antique home with fine artwork and furnishings. Grampa Rose, a kind, gentle man, was never coarse or loud, and I learned a lot from him.

But something was wrong. He developed a nagging cough and started to lose weight. He didn't have any weight to spare, so his weight loss was noticeable to everyone.

One day I was brought to his bedroom. The second I entered his room I knew something was terribly wrong. Grampa was sitting on the edge of his bed wearing dark wool trousers, but all he wore on top was a V-necked, short-sleeved undershirt.

I sat next to him on the bed. It was the first time I had seen him when he was not wearing his long-sleeved shirt. He gave me a kiss on the cheek. He looked so thin and vulnerable. As if to be sure I would remember him, he gave me a present. It was a tall, funny-looking clown made of red, white, and black felt. Its face was hand painted and its limbs had wire inside, allowing them to be bent into any position.

Grampa quietly told me he was going into the hospital. He would be gone a long time, he explained, and I wouldn't be allowed to come and visit. My face felt hot and my throat felt tight as I told him that I would see him when he got out. We both knew my statement did not contain reality. He smiled and gave me another kiss on the cheek. It was the last time I was to see him alive.

He hadn't told me he had tuberculosis. In 1968 TB was usually a death sentence. Afflicted persons were isolated inside sanitariums. Children under age sixteen were considered too susceptible to be around people with active TB. Since I was only twelve, I was not allowed to visit him.

In the following long months, my father would occasionally allow my brother and me to talk to my grandfather with walkie-talkies brought into his room, because there was no phone. We could not see Grampa, for he was too sick to come to the window. But we would stand out in the parking lot and look toward his room, and I would conjure up horrible images of what life must be like inside a TB sanitarium.

My thoughts were jolted back to the present as the car drove over my friends' gravel driveway. It was November and the weather was changeable. I had packed pajamas for cool and warm weather. The room seemed warm, so I wore my lightweight pajamas. Three of us shared a big bedroom on the second floor of the hundred-year-old farmhouse. Soon I was fast asleep.

Suddenly, I awoke. I felt strangely cold and was crying uncontrollably. I rationalized that I must have had a bad dream, yet couldn't recall any dreams at all. And I could not stop crying; tears were streaming down my face. I was inexplicably and utterly sad for no apparent reason. And why was I so icy cold?

Shivering, I silently fumbled through the cold, dark room for my suitcase. I found my warmer pajamas and put them on. My mouth was dry from crying, so I felt my way to the bathroom to get a cup of water. I was careful not to awaken my friends as I returned to the bedroom. I remember thinking how crazy I was acting, yet I continued to cry, filled with inexplicable sorrow. The only thing I could see was the lighted electric alarm clock. It was 1:05 A.M.

As I sat shivering and crying, I noticed an eerie glow forming in the corner. *This is really crazy*, I thought. But as I watched, a strange, warm calm came over me as it began to take the shape of a man from the waist up. It was Grampa Rose!

Amazingly, I was not afraid. There he was, wearing his long-sleeved, white shirt. It had been so long since I had seen him that I found his image comforting. My heart ached as I watched this ethereal image of my beloved grandfather.

It occurred to me that I was seeing Grampa Rose's ghost. And didn't that mean Grampa was . . . ?

But before I could refill my heart with the grief that had awakened me, he spoke, "It's okay, Susie Poosie, everything will be all right. Don't worry, go back to sleep."

As Grampa spoke, my crying and shivering stopped and I was filled with calm. His glow quietly faded away. As if nothing unusual had happened, I crawled under the covers and fell asleep.

In the morning I told my friends about my strange experience. It seemed real, I explained, but it was too weird to have really happened. I rationalized that it must have been a dream.

My friends teased me, saying that I certainly had seen a ghost. But then the youngest girl suddenly exclaimed, "Sue, it couldn't have been a dream. Look, over there in the corner. There are your pajamas and your water cup. You were up last night, so you did see a ghost!"

Could she be right? I wondered. *Had I really seen my grandfather's ghost?*

My parents arrived later that morning to take me to my cousin's birthday party. As I climbed into the back seat of the car, I sensed something was wrong. My parents were unusually subdued. They explained that our plans had changed. We weren't going to my cousin's party.

There was a long silence as I waited for them to tell me the reason, which I already knew. Grampa Rose had died during the night. The words stung as I heard them. As I sat there choking back tears and silently looking out the car window, I grieved that I hadn't seen him in such a long time. And now I'd never get the chance to see him again. My friend was dead.

Finally, after what had seemed like an eternity, I was able to speak. I asked my parents what time Grampa Rose had died. They replied that it was around 1:05 A.M.

It occurred to me that it really had not been very long since Grampa and I had been together. My early morning "dream" wasn't a dream after all.

Grampa knew how devastated I would be over his death. He had come to say goodbye.

Sue Rose-Schmidt
Wonder Lake, Illinois
January 1994

Last Visit

January 1, 1965, the first evening of the new year, began the same as any other. Our two children were sleeping comfortably in the next room and while waiting for my husband to return from his night job I tuned the television to the eleven o'clock news.

As the commentator began to speak I heard someone rapping gently on the window across the room. Rather than ring the doorbell and disturb the children when visiting at night my brother John often announced himself this way. Glancing up I saw it was John.

As always I went to open the door for him. But he wasn't there! I stepped outside and looked around the yard; I even walked out to the sidewalk and glanced up and down the street. Then I noticed that John's car was not parked out front.

Deciding he had remembered he needed a pack of cigarettes or something I went back into the house and put on a pot of coffee so it would be ready when he returned.

The coffee was percolating when the phone rang. It was my brother's wife calling to tell me John had died of a heart attack at 10:55 P.M.—five minutes before he "visited" me.

Diane Marley
Chester, Pennsylvania
January 1967

Grandaddy's Last Visit

When we moved from Cochran, Georgia, to Salem, Virginia, in 1955, it nearly broke my father and mother-in-law's hearts. Our son Edward was then four years old, their youngest grandchild, and although both of them adored him, Edward and his grandfather, Rufus Coody, Sr., were inseparable. To make the move easier for them we promised Grandfather that we would let Edward spend several months with them each summer.

For the next eight years Edward regularly visited with his grandparents as promised. During this time Papa Coody suffered a stroke that left him partially paralyzed on his left side. For a while he was able to get around with the help of a cane but, in his seventies by then, he gradually weakened and finally was confined to a wheelchair. Even so, during the summer when Edward visited him the two had a great time together.

On August 19, 1963, about a month after Edward had returned to Virginia from his latest visit I heard him cry out in his sleep. I looked at the clock as I slipped into my housecoat. It was a little after midnight when I went down the hall to check on my son for now his cries were louder.

As I neared his room I heard him say, "Oh, Granddaddy, don't go! Please don't go!"

The room was dark and unusually cold although the rest of the house seemed quite warm. When I switched on the light I found Edward, now twelve years old, in bed on his knees with his hand stretched out toward something I could not see.

I shook his shoulder gently, saying, "Edward, it's only a dream. Wake up, son."

He shrugged my hand off and crawled to the foot of the bed. "Please don't go, Granddaddy," he sobbed. Finally he collapsed against the foot of the bed, crying as if his heart would break.

I tried to convince him it was only a dream but he shook his head, "He's gone, Mama. I can't see him anymore."

They called from Georgia the next morning to tell us that Papa Coody had died during the night. Then I knew it hadn't been a dream after all.

Papa Coody never visited Virginia when he was alive but he came at the time of his death to tell Edward goodbye.

Barbara S. Guthrie
Salem, Virginia
March 1976

"Packed and Ready"

In early 1968 our son Paul, age twenty-two, came out of Southeast Asia gaunt and exhausted but glad to be alive.

"I really shouldn't be here," he said once. "Only your prayers and the grace of God brought me home from those swamps and jungles."

My husband Charles and I were quite disturbed about Paul's solemn demeanor. He rarely smiled and seemed to have lost the ability to express and appreciate humor.

Nevertheless, during the summer Paul swam, surfed, and sunbathed with his friends. Eventually he registered for the fall term at Santa Monica City College, got himself a part-time job with the Santa Monica Board of Education, and took a little apartment.

His health seemed precarious, however. He had contracted a blood infection in the Vietnamese jungles that wouldn't clear up. Finally, his father and I went to his apartment on Sunday, October 27, 1968, and told him we had come to take him home where we could care for him.

To our surprise, Paul readily agreed. But he asked us to return the next evening when he would be packed and ready. We left, congratulating ourselves on his cooperative attitude.

At 2:40 A.M. that Monday morning I awakened to find Paul standing in our bedroom. I started to get out of bed but Paul raised his hand and said, "Don't get up. I just came to say goodbye."

"Goodbye!" I exclaimed. "Where are you going?"

Paul smiled one of his rare smiles and moved quietly out of the bedroom, down the hall, and out the front door.

The Santa Monica Board of Education permitted Paul to work odd hours because of his tight class schedule. He usually finished work at 11:30 P.M. Then he came to our apartment and rested while I fixed him a sandwich or a meal. About one o'clock he would drive home to Santa Monica and go to bed.

Momentarily forgetting we had seen him in his own apartment earlier that night, I was puzzled only by his statement and the lateness of his visit.

Monday evening we went to get Paul and his belongings. A light was on in his living room but he didn't answer the door. We obtained a key from the building manager and went in. Paul was seated in a chair near the door with his belongings stacked neatly nearby. He was dead.

Later we asked the county coroner the time of his death. "This boy died about 2:30 this morning," he replied.

Genevieve M. DiNoto
Venice, California
July 1971

Stranger at His Side

Early one morning in the summer of 1960 my Aunt Martha Higgens was alone in the laundry that she operated next door to her home. She was in the front part of the building filling the tubs with water when she heard the rear door opening. The hinges screech loudly enough to be heard over the other noise.

My grandfather, who lived just down the street in their little town of Knox City, Texas, had a habit of dropping by about this time in the morning. Without looking around, Aunt Martha called, "Come in, Papa. I'm over here."

Leaning forward to adjust a dial on a machine, she suddenly felt chilled, as if she were in a draft. Turning, she saw Grandfather standing directly behind her. At his side and holding his arm was the strangest-looking man she ever had seen. He was dressed in a neat dark suit and had a pleasant expression on his face. Yet, his body was almost transparent.

Aunt Martha stood motionless and speechless. Then Grandfather approached, touching her on the shoulder.

"Kid," he said, "I must talk to you. Try not to be too upset; these will be our last moments together."

At that instant Aunt Martha realized that his eyes looked strange and glowed weirdly. "Papa, Papa," she whispered, "who is this man?"

"He is . . . uh," Papa paused, as if searching for a name. He continued, "Well, you will understand better if I call him the Death Angel. I have just passed over, and he has come to carry my soul safely across."

"Oh, no!" Aunt Martha cried.

"You must listen," Grandfather continued. "I have only the few moments which this kind gentleman has allowed. I must have your forgiveness. At the instant death came I saw into your heart. You said all these years you had forgiven me, and I believed you. But you never did, did you, Kid?"

When Aunt Martha was a small child, "Kid" had been Grandfather's pet name for her. He had not used it for so long she almost had forgotten it.

Many years ago, as a teen-aged girl, Aunt Martha had fallen in love with a young man of whom Grandfather did not approve. He refused to permit their marriage and caused so much trouble the man finally left town. Heartbroken, Aunt Martha told Grandfather he had wrecked her life and she never would forgive him.

Several years later when she heard the young man had married and had a child, she finally consented to marry an older man whom Grandfather had chosen. Everyone thought she was content if not happy. She had one child, a beautiful daughter, Rose, whom she completely adored.

But when she was twelve, Rose was horribly burned to death. Aunt Martha lay in the hospital for many weeks with hardly the strength or will to live. Grandfather sat at her bedside and heard her cry out in delirium that she never had forgiven him and that she still loved her old sweetheart. Now that Rose was gone she had nothing to live for.

Grandfather realized then what he had done and begged her forgiveness. As she slowly regained her health, Aunt Martha promised he was forgiven, and he believed her.

Now, fifteen years later, he stood in the early dawn with the Death Angel at his side, again pleading for the forgiveness he never had won.

"How did you know?" Aunt Martha sobbed. "I tried to forgive and forget, but in my heart I couldn't. I never meant for you to know. Oh, Papa, you are forgiven now."

The man at Grandfather's side tugged gently on his arm and motioned with his head. Grandfather said, "I must go now. My soul will have peace. Thank you daughter, and goodbye for now."

As he spoke these words the two visitors began to fade slowly from view.

At that instant there was the sound of running feet and voices shouting. "Martha! Martha! Come quickly. Your father has had an attack. Your mother cannot awaken him and we are afraid he is dead."

Aunt Martha turned and said, "Yes, he is gone. There is nothing anyone can do. He was just here to tell me goodbye. I must go and comfort Mother."

The doctor arrived soon and confirmed what Aunt Martha already knew. Grandfather had died quietly in his sleep. He was gone off on a long journey, but he had stopped for a last visit with Aunt Martha.

Lillian Ruth Montgomery
Wichita Falls, Texas
January 1965

The Considerate Spirit

About forty years ago my wife and I lived near Almhurst Road in Westbourne, Bournemouth, England. We were friendly with an elderly couple named Lyons. The husband and I shared a common hobby—photography—and Mrs. Lyons took a great interest in ghost stories, as I do, so we were a good combination.

Mrs. Cherry, a friend to all of us, dropped in one afternoon to chat with my wife. I wasn't busy and they let me join in. The discussion of course centered on our various friends and Mrs. Lyons in particular.

At about 3:30 P.M. my wife glanced at the clock and remarked, "You'll stay to tea, of course?" The invitation was accepted and at that point I suddenly remembered I had a letter that had to catch the early mail. I excused myself and started for the postbox.

It was some distance—around two corners and down another road. On my return trip, whom should I see coming toward me but Mrs. Lyons. I was surprised to see her so far from home as generally she could not get around much.

She had her own ideas about clothes and her garb was quite unconventional. I don't remember exactly what she was wearing but the figure unmistakably was Mrs. Lyons.

As I came closer I said, "Good afternoon, Mrs. Lyons, I'm surprised to see you so far from home. Why not come to my place now you're so near and have tea? Mrs. Cherry is with us and will be glad to see you."

She did not reply but smiled and passed by. I thought this very strange so I turned to watch her. There was no one there! The road was fairly long and open and held no place she could hide nor any gate she might have entered. Was I seeing things?

Back home my wife remarked, "You look as if you have had a fright. What's wrong?"

I told her and Mrs. Cherry what had happened. They thought it must have been a case of mistaken identity. I disagreed, saying I had addressed the woman by name and she had smiled in response. I also reminded them of the peculiarities in Mrs. Lyons's mode of dress.

The afternoon went on and when our guest left we still were wondering about the strange meeting.

The next morning Mrs. Cherry telephoned. She said to me, "You say you saw Mrs. Lyons yesterday? Well, I am sure you did—but possibly not in the flesh—for she was killed in a motor crash early in the afternoon!"

It makes me wonder if the people we see are all real. And why this confrontation in a public road rather than in my home? Perhaps Mrs. Lyons didn't want to frighten my wife and our friend.

J. P. J. Chapman
Poole, Dorset, England
October 1967

Grandfather Smiled

When I was a youngster I lived with my parents Ella and Frank McDonald in the Philippines where my father was employed by the United States government. In the fall of 1940, fearing that war with Japan was imminent, my father sent Mother and me to Merrill, Wisconsin, to live with my grandparents.

I was a teenager then and I attended school there for the remainder of the term. I grew very fond of my grandfather, Joseph Gregson, whom I never had met before this visit. He was not able to speak nor apparently to hear due to a stroke, but he would sit all day rocking in his chair in front of the old-fashioned bay window. I often told him my thoughts and I believed I saw understanding in his eyes. But Grandmother would say, "Don't waste your time. He can't hear you!"

In the meantime, Mother had gone to Chicago to look for work. By late summer of 1941 she had secured employment and a place for us to stay and she sent for me.

Sometime in early September I awakened on my couch-bed in our living room in Chicago to see Grandfather gently rocking in a chair in the center of the room. I called to him but he only smiled at me, then faded slowly from sight.

The next morning Mother told me she had learned that Grandfather had died during the early morning hours—just when I had seen him.

I often wonder why he appeared to me. Was it to show me a smile I had never seen?

Joan Hollingsworth
Laguna Niguel, California
February 1974

No Time to Come In

We had a warm relationship with our seventeen-year-old nephew Brian Hutchison. He was a good fishing companion for my disabled husband Bill and spent a lot of time with us. If I had to be away for a time, he would stay with my husband who is ambulatory only part of the time.

On July 4, 1979, at two o'clock in the morning, I dreamed I heard a loud firm knock at the door. When I opened it I was surprised to see Brian here at that time of the morning.

"Brian," I said, "what are you doing here? Please come in."

He replied, "No, Aunt Leona, I don't have time. I came to say goodbye."

This was so sudden and unexpected, I felt apprehensive and asked where he was going. Brian gave me a warm smile and said, "Oh, away . . ."

"But where are you going?"

Again he smiled that warm smile and said, "Oh, maybe Timbuktu."

"When will you be back?" I persisted.

He looked serious and replied, "I don't know, Aunt Leona."

I felt that he was being evasive and didn't want me to know and this made me sad. Finally he said, "Say goodbye to Uncle Bill. I love you both." Then he turned and left. I was completely bewildered.

At eight o'clock the next morning Brian's mother called to tell us that he had been killed in an auto accident about two o'clock. My dream had told me he didn't have time to come in.

Leona Hutchison
Ogdensburg, New York
August 1987

Blessings
Gifts from the Departed

It seemed appropriate to end this collection with the following stories. What could be more convincing evidence of the continuing existence and concern of the departed than a gift from beyond?

Some of the gifts in these reports are physical items, like rings or money to pay bills; others are less tangible things, like a new ability or protection in a time of danger. But all communicate love, from across an unimaginable distance.

The Apport

When I was a child, one of our neighbors died. Her name was Helen, and she was eighty-nine years old. When my parents and I came to the wake, we saw the old lady serene and beautifully dressed, laid out in a gray casket. On her finger was a ring with a large emerald.

My mother reminded Helen's daughter Millie to remove the ring before the burial. Millie said that Helen wanted her to have the ring, but she thought her mother should wear the ring for the wake. She said that she would remove it before the casket was closed.

At the funeral the next day, Millie was overcome with sorrow and forgot to remove the ring before the casket was closed and locked. The casket was lowered into the grave and the dirt piled in. Millie and her husband stayed at the site until the grave was filled and the floral pieces placed on top.

As they rode home, Millie suddenly remembered that she had not removed the emerald ring from her mother's finger. But it was too late.

The following days were very quiet at our neighbor's house. The family was grieving. We were surprised when Millie pounded on our door. She was wide-eyed and jubilant. She had her mother's emerald ring in her hand. Today was her birthday, and when she awakened, the ring was on her pillow!

All of us had seen her mother's casket closed and locked at the funeral home before the procession to the cemetery. Millie and her husband stayed until the grave was filled with earth. How did the ring get from the dead woman's hand to the daughter's pillow?

This remained a happy mystery. Years later, while studying Spiritualism, I learned that spirits can transport small material items to those they love or are concerned about. These are called "apports." Helen wanted her daughter to have the ring. In a process known only to the spirit world at this time, the ring was transported to Millie's pillow.

At the time, people who heard of the appearance of the ring doubted it. They believed it was another ring Millie's husband bought and put on her pillow, that the funeral director had removed it before he closed the casket, or that the grave diggers took it out.

My family was very skeptical too. But when I saw the radiance of Millie's face, I had no doubt that her mother had, in some way, brought the ring to her daughter's pillow.

Evelyn Thor
Worth, Illinois
August 2000

My Father's Message

My father was seventy years old and semiretired at the time of his death in 1988. I owned a small sign shop, and when the weather was unfit for him to work in road construction, he worked with me. The shop was heated by a wood heater and when either of us came in, we brought a few pieces of wood to let dry for burning later.

About a week after his funeral, I began having the exact same dream three or four times a week. I was working on a sign at the lettering rack and it was very cold outside. My father came in with an armload of wood and put it on the pile. Then he walked over to me, and reached into his coat pocket saying, "If you're not real busy, I have something to talk to you about."

I put down what I was doing, saying, "All right," and turned to face him. Just when he pulled a folded paper from his pocket, I woke up and the dream ended. This went on for weeks, and I mentioned it to no one.

It was about three months later and I was lettering the office hours on a lawyer's office door. I was talking with the lawyer, who was also my friend, and we began talking about my father, whom the lawyer knew well.

I let it slip out about the recurring dream I was having. The lawyer said it sounded as though my father might be trying to relay a message to me. I agreed with him.

The lawyer asked if my father left a will. I told him that he did, and that all his other papers seemed to be in order. He then asked about insurance and I told him that we had not had any on my father. When I completed the job, the lawyer told me he would check on some things concerning my father's death and get back to me later.

A month or so passed after our conversation. Then, early one morning, the phone in the shop rang. It was the lawyer saying he had some good news. (Good news coming from a lawyer was something hard to believe!) He told me he had contacted the company where my father had worked before he died, and found out that they had a ten-thousand-dollar insurance policy on all their employees. The following week my mother had the check from the insurance company. It paid for the funeral and the other expenses that go with a death.

I have had other dreams about my father since then, but after my mother received the check, it was never that same dream as before. I believe my father knew, even in death, that if he did not somehow let us know of the insurance policy, we would never have gotten the money.

Jim Smith
Wadley, Alabama
July 2000

The Blue Sweater

One afternoon in July 1953, I went upstairs to take a nap. The heat was oppressive. I heaved a sigh of relief as I kicked off my shoes and stretched out on the bed.

I think I dropped off to sleep almost at once. I seemed to be in another world. I walked up a winding path and found my mother, Mrs. Sarah G. Vandegrift, waiting for me. I recall that I rushed to her and embraced her warmly.

We sat down together and I noticed that she seemed to be knitting a blue sweater. As we sat there she finished her knitting and held it up for me to see. I thought it was lovely and told her so. It was a beautiful, blue sweater with two white flowers at the neckline on the left side.

She handed it to me saying, "This is for you, dear," and gently pressed it into my hands.

The feel of the sweater was so real that when I awakened I immediately sat up and looked down at my hands. I expected to see the sweater and was surprised when it was not there.

The next day the postman delivered a package from my sister, Ruth Vandegrift, who lived many miles away. It was sent for no special reason, she said later. She had gone shopping and had seen a lovely blue sweater with two white flowers at the neckline and on impulse had sent it to me.

Mother couldn't have told her. She died in April 1945.

Mrs. James W. Everett
St. Petersburg, Florida
July 1954

Mother Insisted

My mother Eula P. James died unexpectedly in March 1968. I had a hard time adjusting to the fact that she was gone. I am an only child with no brothers or sisters to help me bear my grief, and although my husband and children were wonderful and tried to help me through that trying time, I was very lonely. Nobody could take Mother's place.

Mother had played the violin beautifully. I never learned to play this instrument. Although Mother wanted me to take lessons, I wasn't interested. After her death I kept her violin. I couldn't part with it, it was so much a part of her.

At Christmastime when the family gathered together we always sang Christmas carols and Mother had accompanied us on her violin. With the approach of the first Christmas after her death I began to miss her more than ever. I thought sadly, *There will be no playing of carols this year.*

But a strange thing happened. Two nights before Christmas I dreamed Mother told me to get out her violin and play her favorite carol "Silent Night, Holy Night." In my dream I reminded her that I could not play the violin and so could not carry out her request.

On Christmas Eve, after putting some last-minute gifts under the tree, we retired early knowing the next day would be a busy one. During that night I dreamed the same dream I had dreamed the night before. This time, however, Mother insisted I get her violin out of the closet and play it.

Again I said, "I can't play your song; I don't know how to play the violin."

She replied, "You will be able to play; I will show you how."

So when I got up early on Christmas morning I went to the closet where I kept her violin. I took it out of its case, put it under my chin, and laid the bow across the strings. And suddenly I was playing the beautiful Christmas carol "Silent Night, Holy Night." I don't know how I did it or what strings I played on, because I do not know how to play the violin.

Marjorie Jordan
Greenville, Texas
March 1976

Angelic Answers

When I was pregnant with my first child, my mother, Markanne Bantt Larberg, was diagnosed with terminal cancer. She became increasingly weak as the cancer progressed, and when I was in my seventh month of pregnancy, she could hardly talk above a whisper.

I was her only caretaker except for a nurse who came in several days a week to take her vital signs and care for her medical needs. Often in the afternoon I would lay beside my mother and hold her hand, and we talked about the baby who would soon be arriving.

This was her first grandchild and she was excited about seeing the new baby, even though she knew she was dying. We talked about names for the baby and how we would move the furniture to make room for the baby bed, and we planned for the birth.

The week before Christmas I became sleepy and went into my mother's room to lay down with her. She took my hand as she usually did and I fell into a deep sleep.

Three hours later I woke up. The lights from the Christmas tree were blinking on and off, illuminating my mother's face as she lay on her pillow.

Suddenly I saw a bright white light moving around her head. I reached over to awaken her. I realized she was passing over and could not hear my voice.

I began to feel a warmth around my body, as if I was bathed in light, and tears filled my eyes, yet I couldn't cry. I held her hand and lay motionless for a long time before getting up from the bed and calling for medical help. Her time of passing had occurred when I fell asleep.

In the following days, I felt warm and comforted. There was no sadness or mourning as I took care of the funeral arrangements. When I went into the room at night, there was a glow around the bed and I felt warm and secure, so I often slept there. When it was time for the baby to be born, I felt as if my mother were there with me.

The labor was long and hard, but in the last few hours before birth, the contractions went away, rather than becoming stronger. The doctor was mystified at the action of the fetal monitors, so he prepared me for a Caesarean section.

While in the operating room, I began to give birth in a most natural way and the baby was born very quickly. In the last phases of delivery I began to see a white light surrounding the delivery room. At first I thought it was just the operating lights playing tricks on my eyes, but then I realized it was an aura that surrounded me. I knew that my mother was watching over me and helping me deliver my child naturally.

That child was Valerie Christina Larberg, a girl, and three years later I gave birth to another girl—Lara Louise Larberg. It has been thirteen years since my mother's passing, and in these years I have seen a light within the room several times—always in times of crisis or fear.

Once when my daughter was crossing a street, she was in danger of being hit by a car and I screamed at her to stop, but she kept on running. I was too far away to grab her, but

I saw a light surround her and push her out of the way of an oncoming car. She fell in the gutter and started to cry and asked why I had pushed her. I told her I was too far away to have done it, but her guardian angel was there to keep her safe.

I have read about reincarnation and angels, but my only proof is my own experience and the white light I saw.

During my mother's passing I am sure she moved through me to the unborn child and is protecting us as she would if she were alive today.

Thank God for her guiding light.

Ann Larberg
Deland, Florida
August 1994

The Bookmark

I have had many strange proofs that we survive bodily death, but the strangest of all came while I was writing a letter of condolence to my friend Willametta Keffer who lives in Roanoke, Virginia.

Willametta's mother, whom I had never met, died in the summer of 1971 and I decided to write to my pen pal of twenty-five years' standing and try to share with her my thoughts on survival.

As I was writing a prompting came into my mind: "Tell Willametta there is a message from her mother in her mother's Bible." I brushed this aside as imagination until the prompting became more urgent: "Tell her to find the place marked by a crucifix bookmark in the Bible. The message is there."

Trying to ignore the mental promptings I closed my eyes and a picture of a bookmark crucifix flashed into my mind. It seemed to have simulated crocheted or embroidered flowers in its design. This convinced me I should include in my letter the "message" I thought I might have received from her mother. But I had misgivings for I was sure Willametta and her husband Mart, whose respect I value, would think me more than slightly crazy.

Not so! Willametta told me later she read this part of my letter aloud to Mart and he immediately went to get the dead woman's Bible. He returned holding the Bible open at a page marked by a crucifix like the one I had described. On the bookmark was written: "Lo, I am with you always."

Lee Baxter
El Centro, California
April 1974

Grossmutter's Instruction

On January 17, 1973, my mother Mathilda Dixon lay seriously ill in Memorial Hospital in Belleville, Illinois. Her left leg was swollen to twice its normal size. Three specialists we had called in gave us little hope for her recovery.

While I sat heartbroken beside Mother's bed waiting for the end, I heard the voice of my maternal grandmother,

Elizabeth Kopp. I had always called her "Grossmutter" and she in turn had nicknamed me "Kukla" (doll face). Although she had been dead for twenty-five years, I clearly heard her say, "Kukla, you have the power to heal. Lay your hand on your mama."

I stretched out my left hand and it began to tingle as if on fire. I laid my hand on Mother and felt a glow envelop my entire body. Mother sighed and broke out in a sweat that soaked her body with perspiration—and she was miraculously healed! In the days following her leg returned to normal and today she is in perfect health.

Later I remembered how when I was just a child Grossmutter had said I would have strange powers because I had been born with a double caul. Many years later she came in my hour of need to prove it to me.

Dorothy Dixon
Belleville, Illinois
June 1974

A Gift from India

After my divorce in 1973, everything went wrong. I was plagued with health and financial problems and suffered from acute depression. My relatives were thousands of miles away and the friends my husband and I had had quietly disappeared. Almost every day brought new tribulations, which I had to cope with alone, and although I prayed a lot, things continued to get worse. Eventually I became so exhausted and hopeless that I didn't see how I could go on. Finally, one night I prayed, "O Lord, if there is any help for me anywhere in the universe, please send it now."

That night I had a dream. I saw a man with dark hair and a bushy mustache who was dressed in the style of the Victorian era. Somehow I knew he was my paternal grandfather, Andrew MacMillan, who had been killed when my father was a little boy. A civil engineer, Grandfather had gone to India to work on the construction of a railroad and was massacred during a native uprising.

My grandfather didn't move or speak but as he kept looking at me, the words "I will send you a gift from India" popped into my head. As soon as I had received that message he disappeared. I didn't think much about the dream until a few days later.

At that time I had a German shepherd, and while walking him I had met Rosemary Long, who had a little pug. Sometimes we walked the dogs together and chatted.

One morning a few days after my dream she invited me to her house. I had never been in her home before and found it very attractive. She had many rare, beautiful antiques and Oriental objects, but the thing I admired most was her bedroom rug. When I commented on it she told me it was from India.

"Have you been to India?" I asked.

Rosemary nodded, saying, "I was born there."

When she said that, I remembered my dream and a chill ran through me.

She showed me around the bedroom pointing out objects of special interest, then indicated the bed. Some lovely dresses were spread out on it. "I hope you won't be offended," she said, "but I would like you to try them on. I have gained so much weight I can't wear them anymore."

I wasn't surprised to find that the dresses fit me perfectly because I thought they were my grandfather's promised gift. But as it turned out, they were only a small part of it.

Rosemary and I became good friends and she helped me in innumerable ways. Her cheerful companionship, encouragement, practical assistance, and moral support helped to restore my confidence in myself and give me the strength I needed to get back on my feet. I will never doubt that she herself was my "gift from India."

Jean Dobbs
Sarasota, Florida
February 1988

May Ree

My mother, Mary, and my father, Will, had a wonderful marriage. He would have given her anything. He had a pet name for her, and he often called out to her in the big new house he had bought for her. "May Ree," he sang out, and she would reply, "I'm here, dear one."

Nine months after our move my father and older brother went fishing. Usually we all went, but that year my mother and I stayed home. I was thirteen years old and, as they left, my father said in his stern, commanding way, "Take care of your mother."

The week went by and they were due back on the weekend. I am a very sound sleeper, but on that Friday night I woke and could not get back to sleep. I got up, looked at the full moon, got back into bed, and was just about to doze off when I heard my fathers' voice say, "Elizabeth," in a demanding way. (He had always called me "Punkins," never my birth name.) I sat up, listened hard, and lay back down, thinking I might have dreamed this.

Again I heard his voice, so I got out of bed and looked down at the driveway for his car. Nothing. Then I went back to sleep. Awakened by the phone ringing, I ran down the hall. My mother was there saying, "No, no, no!" I took the phone and it was my brother, but I already knew that my father was dead.

The funeral was a nightmare for my mother. I felt numb but found myself helping with the funeral and the wake at the new house. Three months later I was doing my homework in our kitchen and my mother came in. The phone rang and she went into the hall to answer it. I heard her voice lift up as she said, "Oh my, how are you?"

I sighed with relief and assumed it was my brother, who had joined the navy. I heard her say, "But where are you?" and then silence. She came back and sat down, eyes sparkling, and said, "That was your father."

"But how could that . . . ?" I started.

"How could it be?" she said, and started sobbing. "But I know it was him."

"What did he call you?" I asked

She answered, "Why 'May Ree,' of course, and he said I had not paid the mortgage for three months and that we were going to lose the house."

"Is that all he said?" I asked.

"No, he said I was to go to the bank tomorrow, and then he just faded away."

I told her that she should talk with our new neighbor, a banker, about this. She went over to his home, then came back saying that she was to go to his office in Los Angeles and he would do what he could.

He was the head of the new Federal Housing Authority loan division. He gave us a loan, caught up the payments, and reduced the mortgage from ninety dollars to twenty-five dollars a month. Then I realized father was watching over his beloved wife and that life after death was absolutely true.

Some people I told this story to shook their heads, but I just laughed. My father was a design engineer for AT&T, so it makes sense that he would phone my mother.

That phone call strengthened my spiritual beliefs. I was certain from that moment on that prayer heals and that we have divine protection.

Elizabeth Lockwood
Salem, Oregon
October 1996

Clara!

I think I have telepathic powers. If I concentrate my thoughts long and hard on a friend or relative, I always end up receiving a phone call or a letter. This has happened a number of times, so it can't be just coincidence. But the incident that occurred on the night of December 23, 1976, was most unusual.

My husband Tom was fighting for his life in the intensive care unit of Queen Mary Hospital in Hong Kong after having suffered a multiple heart attack at a sports stadium the day before. Back at home, my daughter Tanya was running a temperature of 103 degrees. Our family doctor diagnosed influenza and assured me that she would be fine. But I was afraid as I sat beside her cot applying ice to her burning forehead.

Finally, exhausted, I lay down to rest, my mind picturing Tom's life ebbing away. "Oh, God," I pleaded, "help me!"

I thought of my friend Clara Tellis and wished she were with me. Her optimism and bright chatter would dispel my fear.

She was always there when we needed her and when one of us was ill she would call with her special soup made from fragrant herbs. Clara was a good friend and neighbor. Kind, helpful, and generous, she was a frequent visitor from the day our daughter was born. She became Tanya's godmother and her second "Mommie" who took her for walks, taught her songs and rhymes, and made her pretty clothes.

"Clara, I'm afraid," I whispered as I felt sleep slowly overcoming me. "If only you were here!"

As I tossed and turned, I felt a gentle touch on my head and peace filled my whole being. "Don't worry, Helene," someone said. "Everything will be all right."

Clara was standing beside my bed, speaking in her kind and soothing voice. I recognized the special way she pronounced my name.

"Clara!" I called, overjoyed. I stretched out my hand to grasp hers but felt emptiness instead.

"Clara, is it really you?" I asked. There was no answer.

I woke up. For a moment I thought I had been dreaming. Then in the dimness I saw Clara hovering over Tanya.

"Clara!" I called again, my heart pounding. "How did you get in?"

She said nothing, only smiled.

"Clara, wait! Don't go yet!" I implored her.

I stopped short. This was impossible—Clara couldn't be in our room. She had died unexpectedly of a stroke three years earlier.

My heart racing, I sprang out of bed and dashed over to my daughter. I felt her forehead. The fever had broken and she was sleeping soundly.

I felt peace. Clara had promised everything would be fine. When Tom recovered too, it was.

Helene C. Chew
Vancouver, British Columbia, Canada
February 1987

Life's Heart

For the second time in as many days I felt a presence in the room. But when I turned my head I was alone.

Sitting in the kitchen trying to juggle my income to cover current expenses, and still have the nine hundred dollars I needed for my son's college tuition, was a real challenge. After going over everything for the fifth time I was still four hundred dollars short.

Since my husband's sudden death the year before, in 1963, I had managed to keep our son in college. He was taking extra courses to finish early and also cooking at a diner on weekends.

This time there seemed no way to manage. Putting my head in my arms on the table I gave in to despair.

Suddenly I felt the warmth again and a presence in the room as I had felt the previous days. I sat quietly and gave myself up to the wonderful feeling that enclosed me.

Maybe I felt the words. I don't know. "Zoe! Zoe!" said my husband's voice.

This can't be, I thought. *He is dead. He is gone.*

Again I heard, "Zoe. Zoe." I knew it was his voice; I heard it—maybe in my head.

"Neil, is it really you?" I asked.

"Yes. I'll be with you as long as you need me. Look in *The Prophet*, page twelve and then page eighty. I love you. I'll always love you. So long." And then all was still.

I sat for some time in the warm glow repeating, "I love you. I love you. So long!" Our special words for goodbye. Then I was on my feet looking around frantically. The experience was so vivid I searched the house, calling Neil's name.

Finally, I sank in a chair, my head whirling with questions and disbelief. I doubted my senses. Had I dozed? Had the stress of the last year been too much for me?

I forced myself to relax and think, hoping for Neil's return. Gradually, as I relaxed, I let my thoughts drift to the love we had experienced. Talking all night. Sharing our most intimate thoughts. Laughing sometimes at the many struggles over the years. Just being together! The physical ache; the feeling that a part of my body was gone.

Now, more relaxed, I walked slowly into the living room and took from the bookcase our worn copy of *The Prophet* by Kahlil Gibran. My thoughts were on the many times we had read certain parts to each other, along with the Bible, when we faced a crisis in our marriage, or needed comfort when we had problems that seemed too big for us to solve.

I stood holding *The Prophet* in my hands for a moment, then opened it to page twelve. The underlined words were the ones we had read many times after a close family member had died:

"All these things shall love do unto you that you may know the secrets of your heart, and in that knowledge become a fragment of Life's Heart."

Life's heart! Neil's heart!

I stood for a long time amazed at how simple and wonderful the words were: Life's heart. Neil's heart.

Then scarcely aware of what I was doing, I turned to page eighty. Four crisp one-hundred-dollar bills marked the place and, underlined many years before, were these words:

"For life and death are one, even as the river and the sea are one."

Zoe H. Crow
Marion, North Carolina
June 1987

Afterword

FATE's collection of survival evidence is ever-growing. If you have had a personal experience like the ones in this book, or if you would like information on subscribing, we encourage you to write us at:

FATE magazine
PO Box 460
Lakeville MN 55044

GET MORE AT **LLEWELLYN.COM**

Visit us online to browse hundreds of our books and decks, plus sign up to receive our e-newsletters and exclusive online offers.

- **Free tarot readings • Spell-a-Day • Moon phases**
- **Recipes, spells, and tips • Blogs • Encyclopedia**
- **Author interviews, articles, and upcoming events**

GET SOCIAL WITH **LLEWELLYN**

Find us on Facebook
www.Facebook.com/LlewellynBooks

Follow us on
twitter
www.Twitter.com/Llewellynbooks

GET BOOKS AT **LLEWELLYN**

LLEWELLYN ORDERING INFORMATION

Order online: Visit our website at www.llewellyn.com to select your books and place an order on our secure server.

Order by phone:
- Call toll-free within the U.S. at 1-877-NEW-WRLD (1-877-639-9753)
- Call toll free within Canada at 1-866-NEW-WRLD (1-866-639-9753)
- We accept VISA, MasterCard, and American Express

Order by mail:
Send the full price of your order (MN residents add 6.875% sales tax) in U.S. funds, plus postage and handling to: Llewellyn Worldwide, 2143 Wooddale Drive Woodbury, MN 55125-2989

POSTAGE AND HANDLING:

STANDARD: (U.S., Mexico & Canada)
(Please allow 2 business days)
$25.00 and under, add $4.00.
$25.01 and over, FREE SHIPPING.

INTERNATIONAL ORDERS (airmail only):
$16.00 for one book, plus $3.00 for each additional book.

Visit us online for more shipping options. Prices subject to change.